The Making of the Pope

By Tony Spina

Additional Text by Dawson Taylor

With a Foreword by John LaFarge, S. J.

New York • A. S. Barnes and Company • London

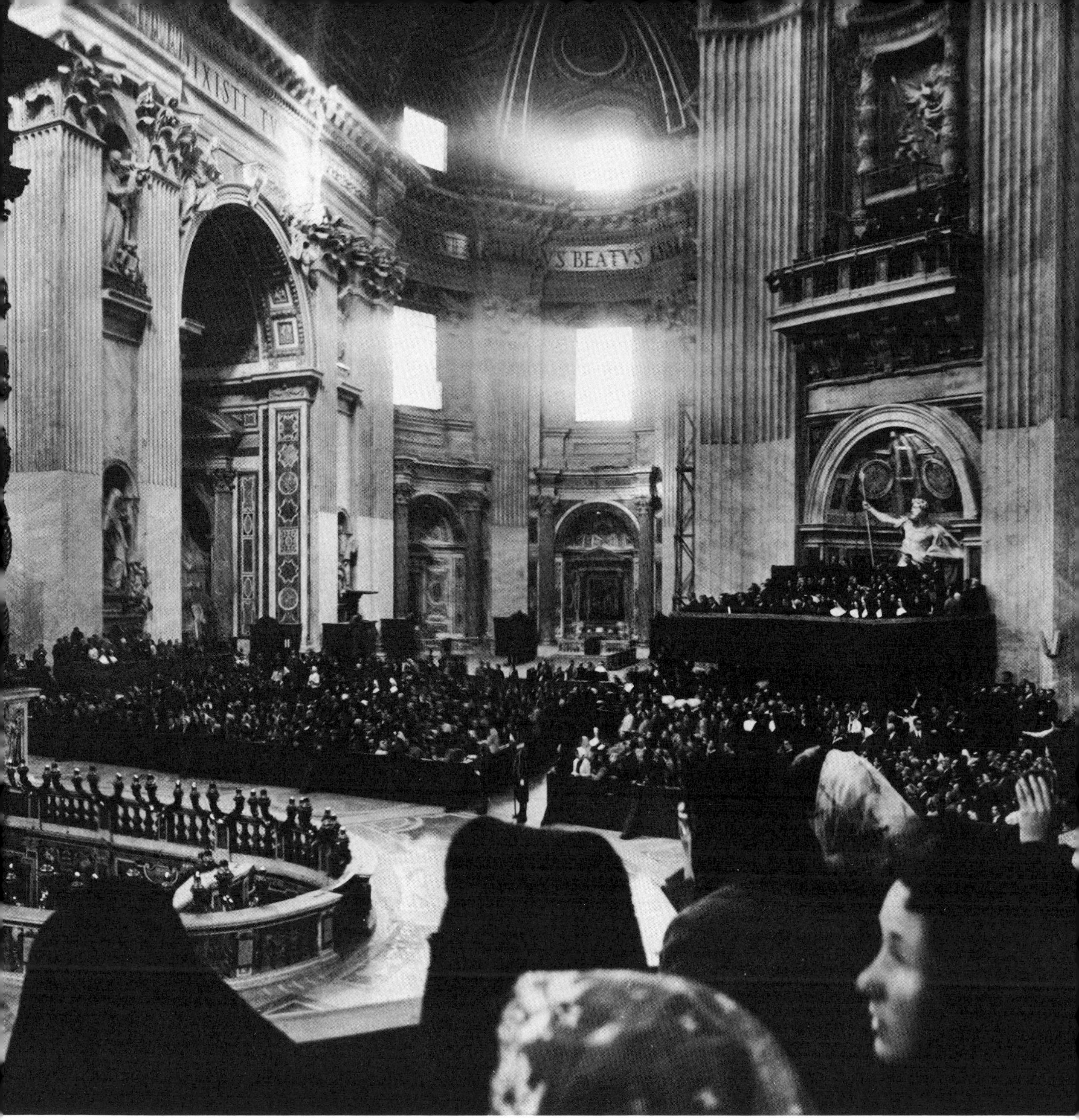

The Making of the Pope

© 1962 by A. S. Barnes and Company, Inc.
Library of Congress Catalog Card Number: 62-14977

9625
Printed in the United States of America

Foreword

SOME OF US have often wondered why there is such a particularly keen popular interest in the election of a Supreme Pontiff of the Catholic Church.

One good reason for such interest lies in the fact that there is nothing like such an election anywhere in the world. The determination of the choice for a Roman pontiff has repeated itself in continuous line for nearly 2,000 years. Sometimes this momentous choice has occurred in complete calm and freedom, sometimes under turmoil and circumstances of extreme political pressure. Yet whenever such pressure is brought to bear upon the free functioning of the Church, it has aroused intense resentment. For, from the very nature of the papal election, it is something that should occur in complete absence of any pressure from outside influence of any description.

In the choice of a Pontiff, the Church acts, so to speak, from its inmost nature, as a divinely instituted society through which the Holy Spirit teaches and sanctifies mankind. Hence the Church's anxious desire that worldly influence and any form of personal ambitions should be excluded as far as is humanly possible from such a momentous choice.

The Pontiff's shoulders bear a terrific burden of responsibility. The burden is tremendous because of the duties that attach to the office itself: the threefold work of teaching the sacred message bequeathed to His Church by its Founder, Jesus Christ; of governing and administrating the world-flock entrusted to him, and finally, the work of sanctifying our human kind. This means transmitting to them or seeing that others transmit to them the stream of sacramental graces.

The performance of such a function presents an equally tremendous challenge to all the personal resources of any man who is shouldered with its execution at any time, but in a most special way at the present moment, when the Church of God must find its way through violent storms of political and ideological opposition. One of the marvels of our age is the lofty character and intelligence of each of the Popes who, each in his own fashion, has come to face the revolutionary changes of the last century and a quarter, such men as Popes Pius IX, Leo XIII, St. Pius X, Benedict XV, Pius XI, Pius XII, and our present Pope John XXIII. Yet each of these men has been selected for a job of heroic struggle and hard work even up to death in what is popularly called the evening of life, at a time when most people retire from the responsibilities of any high office, and seek a few years of undisturbed peace and quiet.

We shall place the election in better focus, if we remember just *who* is elected, and *by whom* he is chosen. The Pope is not some sort of detached super-being, hovering freely above the Church. He is simply the Bishop of Rome, the primatial diocese of the universal Church, and his various prerogatives—as mentioned above—all flow from the prerogatives attached to the Bishop of Rome. He has, therefore, the ordinary functions and privileges of any bishop of a diocese, plus the special functions that were enjoyed by Rome's first bishop, the Apostle Peter, and Peter's successors in that office.

Again, he is not elected by membership of the entire Church—nor even by all the Bishops of the Church—but only by a select body of selectors, the so-called College of Cardinals. For Americans it is interesting that actually the President of the United States is elected in the same way: by the College of Electors, who, by our Constitution, meet at a certain time and spot every four years and cast their votes for the President. True, the members of the Electoral College of the United States renounced their individual judgment early in our history, and became mere instruments to register the choices already made by the people. Yet *legally* they still remain electors, and at each presidential election dissenting State politicians can frighten their enemies by threatening to persuade the electors to go off "on their own."

It is generally accepted that the American College of Electors owes its origin to Daniel Carroll, of Maryland, an American Catholic statesman of the time, who in turn derived the idea from the Roman College of Cardinals.

Two elements strike the popular eye in the election of the Pope. These are openness and secrecy. Openness, because the persons who make the choice are exposed to full view of the entire world, and are rigidly safeguarded against even the shadow of any pressure from any source whatsoever, save the promptings of their own personal judgment and conscience. They can receive no message, send no messages, and the most elaborate precautions are taken to keep them entirely to themselves during the period of their deliberations. The same precautions act for the absolute privacy and secrecy of their proceedings. The only persons with whom they may communicate are those of their own number, and their persons and deliberations are placed under lock and key and armed guardianship during these days of choice. Most of the electors are persons well on in years, so proper though plain provision—lodging, food, medicine, etc.—is offered for the time of their exile from the highly inquisitive world. But the grimly businesslike armed guard appearing in the accompanying photographs symbolizes the firmness of the Church's position on electoral seclusion and secrecy. And—to the delight of the Roman press correspondents of the world—the first announcement of the fact of a successfully completed election is made through the wisps of white smoke from burned ballots that ascend from the famous chimney-pipe in the Hall of Election, the signal that is immediately transmitted through the entire world.

The magnificent collection of photographs that comprise this superb album speaks for itself. They bring home to us in most appealing fashion the radiant personality of our present beloved Pontiff, Pope John XXIII. Pope John's inmost prayer and constant exhortation is that the current World Council of the Bishops of the Catholic Church, Vatican II, which opened on October 11 of 1962, may bring peace and unity to a divided humanity, torn by national and racial hate, and by religious dissension, and the grim specter of fear hovering over the entire globe. May the pictures of peace and freedom that this album presents inspire all who examine it to join with Pope John in his prayer for human unity.

— Reverend John LaFarge, S.J.

Nihil Obstat: /s/ Matthew P. Stapleton
 Diocesan Censor
Imprimatur: † Richard Cardinal Cushing
 Archbishop of Boston
Date: October 31, 1962

Contents

	Page
Foreword	v
How This Book Came to Be	15
The Election of the Pope	27
The Development of the Papacy	42
The State of the City of the Vatican	49
The Gathering of the Cardinals	75
The Pontificate of Pope John XXIII	117
Highlights of the Life of Angelo Giuseppe Roncalli	135
Previous Ecumenical Councils	137
List of Popes	138
Bibliography	140

The Making of the Pope

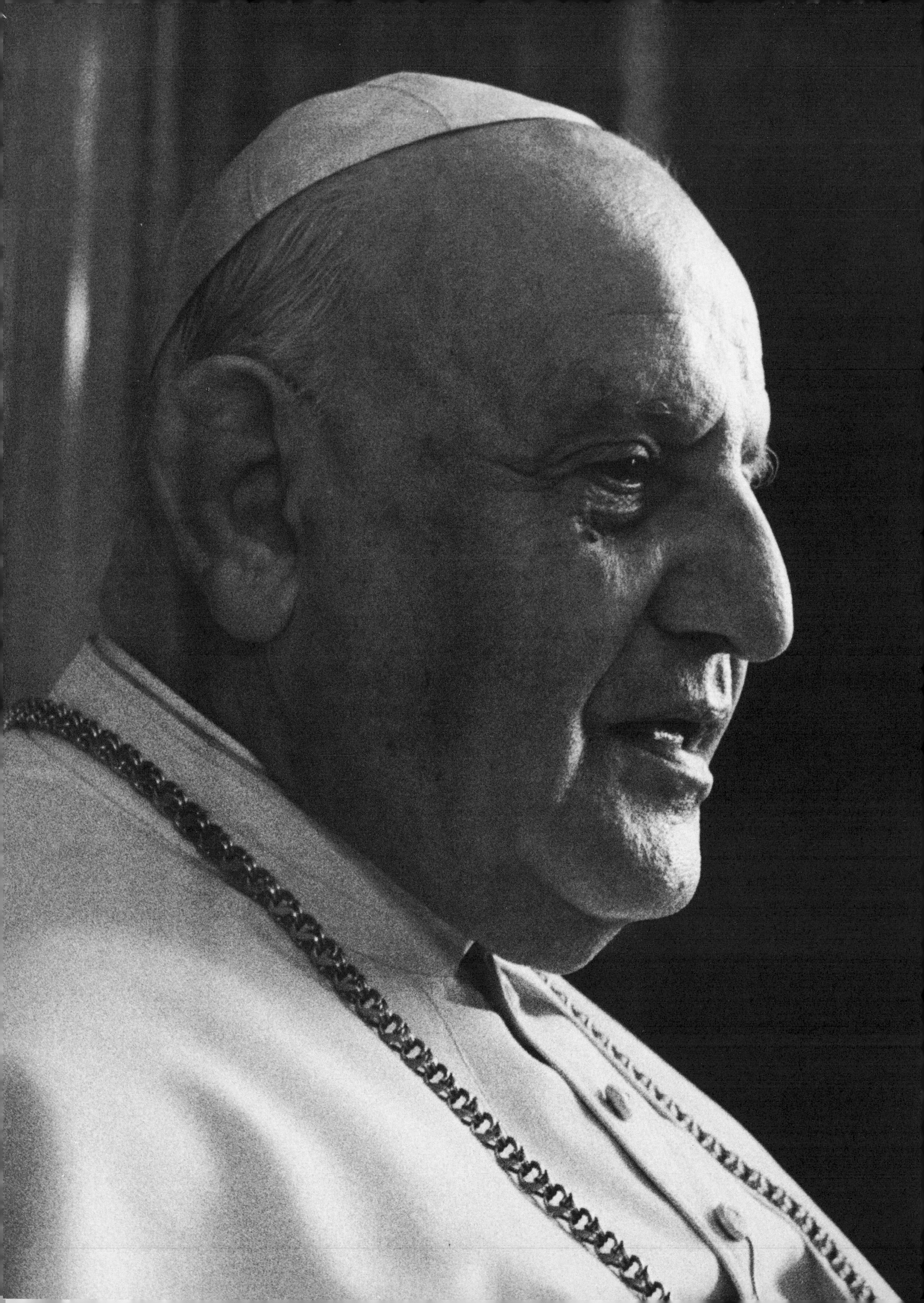

How This Book Came To Be

"The Holy Father is ready."

With these five simple words began a two-hour period that represented the greatest experience of my life. For 105 minutes I was in the presence of a great man—a warm, friendly, generous man, who is also the spiritual leader of five hundred million people.

I had arrived in Rome on Sunday, May 8, 1960, hoping for the opportunity to photograph the Pope. A year and a half earlier, I had been in Rome on that historic occasion in October, 1958 when Angelo Giuseppe Roncalli had been elevated to the highest office in the Roman Catholic Church. I had followed every moment of that awesome time, photographing everything around me—the dignitaries of the Church, gathered to elect a successor to the great Pope Pius XII; the anxious, excited throngs in St. Peter's Square; the columns of smoke that signalled the progress of the conclave to the crowds; the thrilling moment when the identity of the new Pope became known.

Now I had returned to seek the fulfillment of my fondest dream—to take a series of pictures of the Pope in his palace, to complete the story that had begun for me seventeen months before. I knew that no photographer had ever been permitted to take pictures of Pope John XXIII in the palace, except the Pope's own photographer, Felici, but I wanted the chance more than anything else in the world. Kind hands had opened the way and smoothed the path before me; in advance of my coming, a letter from the Most Reverend John F. Dearden, Archbishop of Detroit, to Archbishop Martin J. O'Connor, Rector of the North American College and President of the Pontifical Commission for Motion Pictures, Radio and Television at the Vatican, had turned the magic key. Archbishop O'Connor had put me in touch with Monsignor Andrew M. Deskur, secretary of the Commission, and on Monday morning, when I telephoned Monsignor Deskur, with a mixture of fear and hope, he greeted me cordially. He was not sure my request would be granted, but he promised to present it to the Maestro di Camera. He would telephone me as soon as he had an answer.

For the next two days I waited anxiously, hardly daring to leave the telephone in my room at the Savoy Hotel. On Wednesday Monsignor Deskur called me. He was sorry that he had not yet received a reply from the Maestro di Camera. He asked how long I planned to stay, and when I told him I expected to leave the following Sunday, he expressed regret. He thought the Pope would see me, if I could stay on a little longer.

If I could stay on! I did not tell him that I would have stayed on a month if that were necessary to see the fulfillment of my dream. I answered politely that I thought I could arrange to stay on. He assured me he would try to make the arrangements, but he cautioned me to hold myself available, because he could give me only a few hours notice when the appointment was finally made.

So I prepared myself for a long and anxious wait. But a pleasant surprise was in store for me. At two o'clock the very next afternoon, Monsignor Deskur called again, very excited. I was in luck—the Pope could see me that evening promptly at five o'clock. I would be given five minutes in which to take my pictures, so I was to come well prepared. Everything was arranged with the greatest punctuality. I was to meet Monsignor Deskur at the Palazzo San Carlo promptly at four o'clock, and we were to arrive at the Vatican Palace at exactly four-thirty.

Now I embarked on the busiest two hours of my life. I had no idea what conditions I would be faced with in this enterprise. What would be the arrangement of the room, the lighting conditions, the area in which I would have to work? What equipment should I take? Should I rely on whatever lighting would be available or should I take along lighting equipment? I had to trust largely to instinct in making my decisions and pray that my instincts would guide me well. At last I decided. I would rely on the existing light, hoping thus to catch Pope John completely at his ease. I hoped to bring away with me on film the best pictures ever made of the Pontiff. I selected two thirty-five millimeter cameras and a special 140-degree, extra-wide-angle camera. I loaded one camera with color film and two with black-and-white, and I was ready for the crowning experience of my career as a photographer.

By the time I had finished my preparations, I had barely enough time to get a taxi and make my four o'clock appointment with Monsignor Deskur. He was waiting for me outside the Palazzo when I arrived, and after I had introduced myself, he led the way to the Vatican Palace. We went by way of the back streets, around St. Peter's Basilica, through passages and doorways that were colorful and impressive. I wished we could have lingered a few minutes to take it all in, but I could only hurry along beside my guide.

Monsignor Deskur was very kind. He insisted on carrying some of my equipment, in spite of my protests. He asked me if I knew the Very Reverend Father Celestin J. Steiner, Chancellor of the University of Detroit, who has been one of the most farsighted educators in televison programming. He was delighted when I told him that Father Steiner was an old friend.

Pope John's private study in the Vatican Palace.

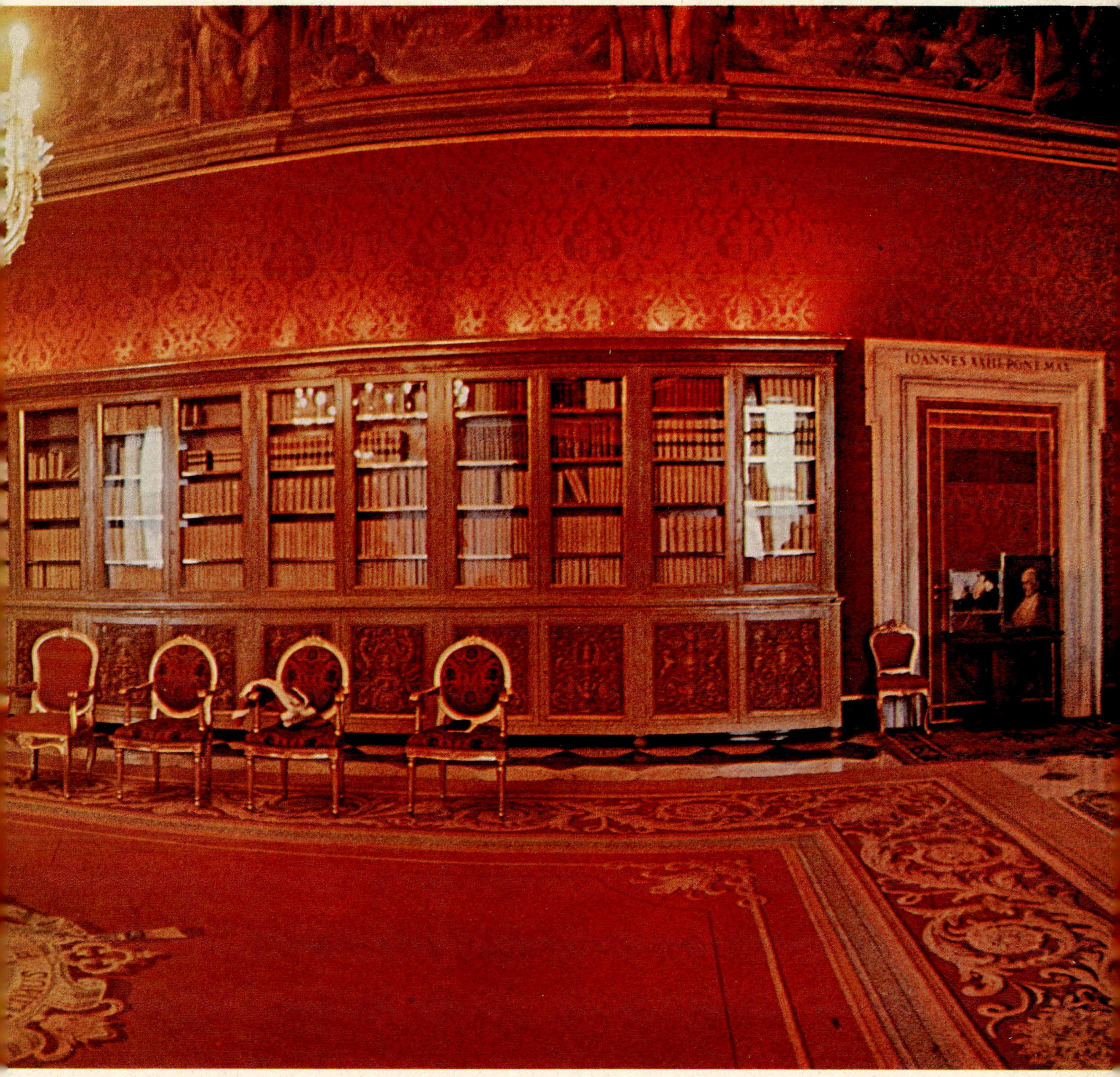
IOANNES XXIII PONT MAX

I did not know quite how to introduce the subject that was heavy on my mind. I had never met a Pope before, and I had no idea of the proper etiquette. Finally I found the courage to explain my predicament.

"What do I do?" I asked.

Monsignor Deskur smiled. "Just kneel and kiss the Papal ring," he said—then he added kindly, "and don't worry about it."

It was a wonderful ten-minute walk. At intervals, as we passed through the gates of buildings, Swiss guards brought their lances to rigid salute, and Monsignor Deskur acknowledged the courtesy by tipping his hat. At the Palace he led me directly to the third floor, where he pointed out to me an old mural depicting the ancient world. He wanted to be photographed beside this mural, one of his favorite paintings. I took his picture and promised to present a print to Father Steiner.

From here we went down to the second floor, and he directed me to a large and beautifully appointed room, where I was to meet Monsignor Igino Cardinale, at that time engaged in the Secretariat of State for Ordinary Affairs and now Chief of Protocol of the Vatican State, who would take me to Pope John. Monsignor Deskur then left me. In the ten minutes that I waited, I had ample opportunity to study this magnificent room. I estimated that it was about forty feet wide, eighty feet long, and at least eighteen feet in height. I was told by one of the guards that this was the room in which the Pope met with his "cabinet" to deal with affairs of state. The walls were hung with tapestries and paintings, and the ceiling was encrusted with flakes of gold said to have been brought by Christopher Columbus from the New World. Against one of the walls was a beautifully decorated throne surmounted by a canopy.

At a few minutes before five, Monsignor Cardinale arrived and greeted me warmly. He spoke English well, and he told me, as we walked together toward the Pope's private study, that he had lived in Brooklyn. A walk through four large rooms brought us at last to a small anteroom, where we were to wait to be called into the Pope's study. Our wait was very brief. Promptly at five o'clock, the door on the other side of the anteroom opened, and Monsignor Loris Capovilla, His Holiness' special secretary, announced: "The Holy Father is ready."

Monsignor Cardinale led the way into the Pope's study and I followed. I hoped he would not see how nervous I was, but I was sure he could hear the pounding of my heart as I came into the presence of the Holy Father. Almost automatically, I followed him across the room, to the desk where Pope John was standing. I knelt and kissed the Papal ring, without a word, and began immediately the work I had come for. I prepared the cameras and took many photographs, in complete silence. Only after I had taken a dozen pictures, switching from camera to camera, did I feel relaxed enough to look about me and to study the Pope. He is of medium height, I judged about five feet seven inches, but his bulk gives one the impression that he is shorter. He was dressed in a white cassock, with a white skull-cap on his head.

While I was working, he was smiling in a quizzical manner. I did not realize

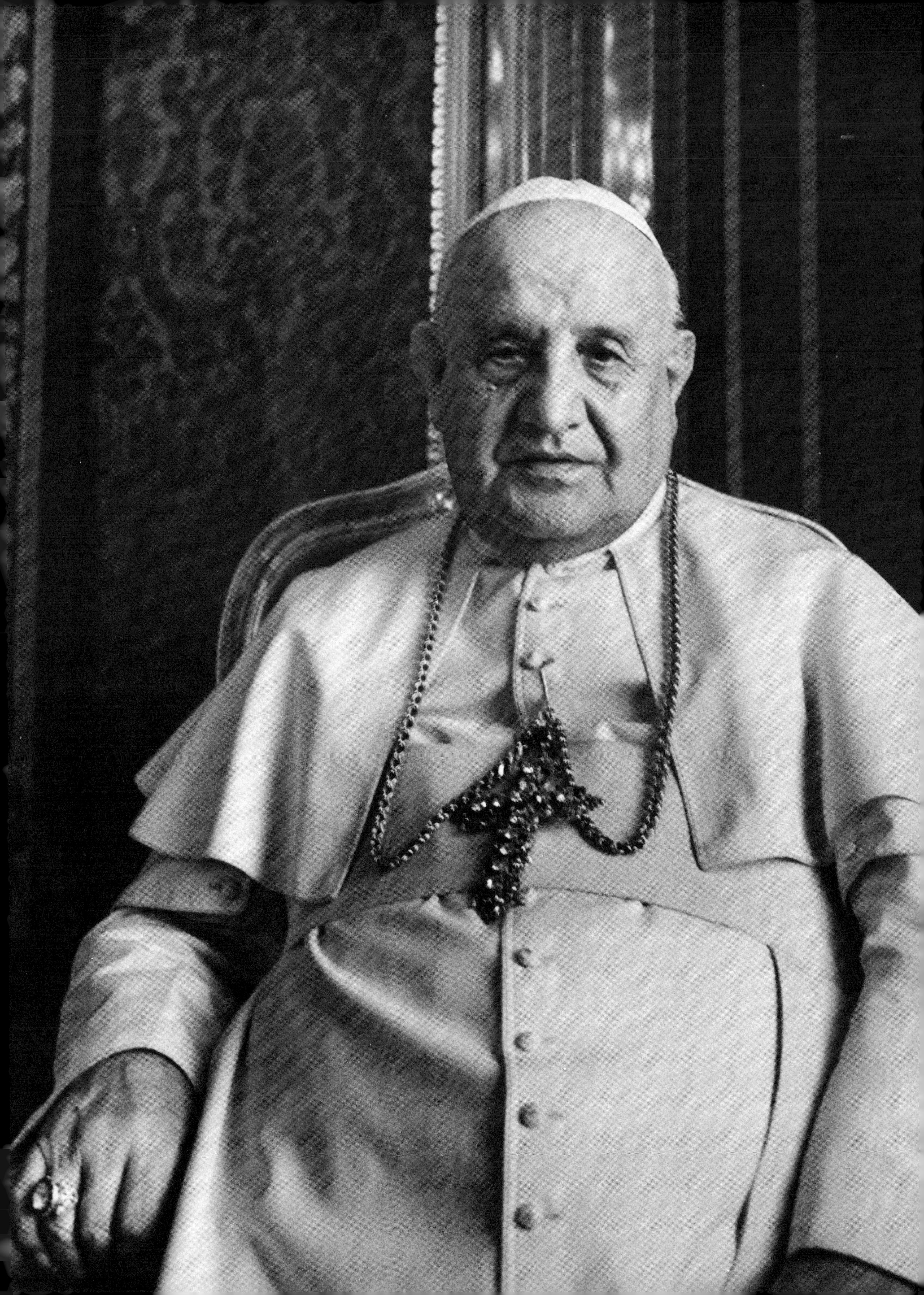

why until Monsignor Capovilla asked me where I wanted the Pope to stand. He explained that the Pope was waiting for me to set up my lights and he would then take any pose I desired. I held up the camera I was using and explained that there would be no lights, that I would use the normal lighting of the room, and that I had already in fact taken a dozen pictures. I could see that Pope John was impressed and amazed. He turned to his secretary and asked: "What kind of a camera is that?"

I explained that with a combination of fast lenses and fast film, I could depend on the available light in the room to give me what I wanted.

The Pope's face brightened with a warm smile. "I like pictures like that," he said.

The Pope's private study seemed even larger than the first room I had entered on this floor—about fifty feet by a hundred feet, I thought. A huge crystal chandeleir was suspended from the center of the ceiling. The walls were of crimson brocade, and one wall was lined with books in glass-fronted shelves. The thick carpet was of crimson and gold.

The Pontiff was standing beside his desk, which was bare except for a large gold cross, a small lamp, and an ornament of glass, which was probably used as a paperweight. Behind his desk hung a brilliant tapestry that depicted an episode in the life of Christ. It was the Holy Father's favorite tapestry, I was told, and I made certain that it was in the background as I took my photographs.

Several times the Pope expressed his delight at the pictures that needed no blazing lights, and I thanked the instinct that had prompted my decision.

"Would you like me to wear my red cape?" he asked me. I said I would and his valet immediately brought the brilliant cloak.

While I worked Pope John talked pleasantly to me, and I was grateful for his warmth and understanding. "Where do you come from?" he asked.

"Detroit," I answered; "where the automobiles are made," I explained.

"Yes, I know," he smiled. Then, "Spina," he said, "that's an Italian name."

I explained that my parents had come from Italy in 1898.

The session had now gone far past the few minutes that had been allotted to me, and I started to put away my equipment. The Pope gestured to me with his right hand.

"Stay," he said cordially, and I was very happy to obey.

The Pontiff spoke to his secretary, who explained to me that a sitting had been scheduled for the great Italian sculptor Giacomo Manzu, who was completing a head of the Pope. The sculptor, who had been waiting in an anteroom, was summoned, and he came in carrying the half-finished head modelled in clay. He set the figure up on a stand near the window and the Pontiff took his place on a throne that had been set up for the sitting. The valet slipped a purple pillow beneath the Pontiff's feet, and the great man relaxed in his chair.

I asked Monsignor Cardinale if I could photograph the sitting.

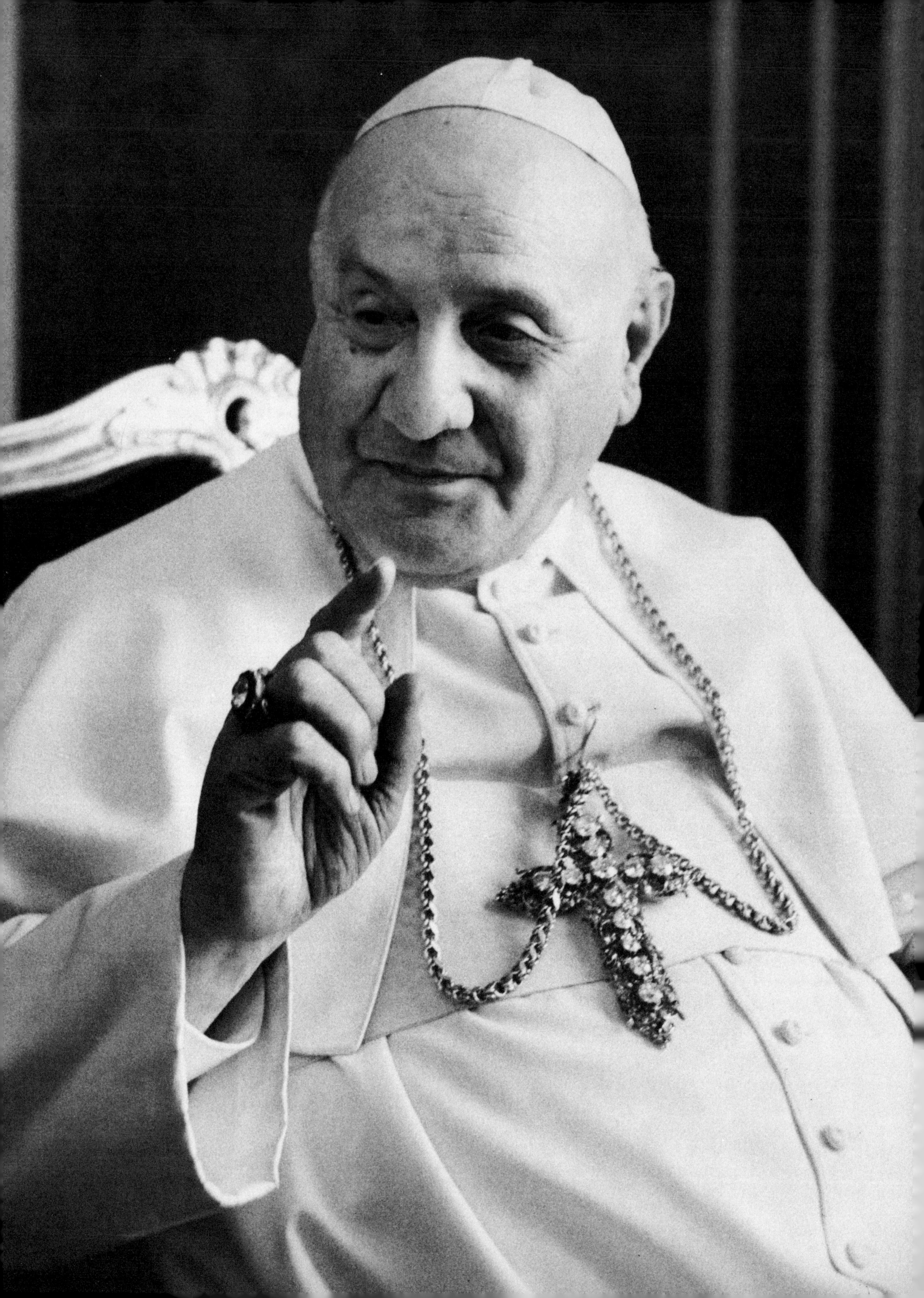

"The Pope said you could stay," he replied.

"But he didn't say I could take pictures."

The Monsignor smiled. "The first time Manzu came here he was so nervous, he collapsed, and we had to revive him on that divan," he confided in me. I could sympathize with the sculptor, I thought.

As unobtrusively as possible I worked my way over to the other side of the room with my cameras, and took my first shot with the wide angle camera. The Pope smiled and nodded almost imperceptibly, but enough to put me at ease and to let me know he approved. Made bolder by this sign of approval, I approached to within three feet and took some superb close-up shots. The Pontiff motioned to the beautiful gold and diamond cross that glittered on his chest.

"Be sure you don't take half the cross," he admonished me. "Take either above or below it, but don't take half of it."

I could see that the Pope was thoroughly enjoying our session of picture-taking, and I was overjoyed. He was conversing easily with me, following every move with the different cameras. I exhausted the film in all the chambers, and I moved to the other side of the room to reload. Monsignor Cardinale nodded approvingly.

"You certainly seem to be getting along well with the Holy Father," he said. Then he smiled. "You know, the Holy Father has an Irish priest who is teaching him English. We're all waiting to see if he learns to speak with an Irish brogue."

While Manzu worked, I turned my attention to the room itself. I wanted to capture the beauty of it on film, and I took all of it, sweeping the wide expanse with my panoramic camera, and taking the details with my thirty-five millimeter cameras. When the sitting was finished, I took a few shots of the sculptor with the clay model.

When Manzu had gone, the Pope called in his personal photographer. He showed Felici the wide angle camera and asked him if he had ever seen a camera like it. The photographer replied that he knew of such cameras but had not been able to get one. I promised that I would send him one when I got back to America, and the Pope smiled and nodded his approval.

The Holy Father showed me two small paintings on a table in one corner of the room. One was a miniature of Pope Leo XIII and the other a painting of the dome of St. Peter's Basilica.

For a few minutes we relaxed in pleasant conversation. Monsignor Cardinale told the Pope that I had covered the conclave of 1958 that resulted in his election. He seemed pleased and asked me if I would send him a set of the photographs I had made.

While we were talking, I thought that this day would be perfect if I could only come away with a picture of myself with the Pope. At last I found the courage to ask Monsignor Cardinale if the Holy Father would allow Felici to photograph us together. The Pope received my request warmly. He directed the arrangements, motioned to me to stand beside him, and asked the Monsignor to pose with us.

Don't take half the cross," Pope John admonished Photographer Spina. "Take above or below it." The photographer followed instructions.

The Pope sits for a sculpture portrait, as Monsignor Cardinale looks on.

The Vatican photographer had with him one of his own cameras with an electronic flash, which he used for this picture.

My meeting with Pope John, which I had been warned could not take more than five minutes, had now lasted more than an hour and a half, and I prepared to leave.

"Before you go," said the Pope, "I want to give you something." He extracted from a drawer of his desk a small red box, about three inches square. On it was a crest of gold, with the Pope's emblem. Nervously I opened it. Inside was a silver medallion bearing an embossed likeness of the Pontiff.

HOW THIS BOOK CAME TO BE 23

I could hardly speak, so moved was I. "I shall treasure this always," I said.

I knelt for the Pope's blessing, and he blessed the rosaries I had brought with me, and a St. Christopher's medal I carried always in my wallet. I kissed the ring, and my wonderful meeting was over.

Monsignor Cardinale escorted me to the door.

"Can you find your way out?" he asked. I nodded and said goodbye to him.

When I returned to America, I was anxious to prepare the set of photographs I had promised the Pope. I went to seek the advice of Archbishop Dearden, and with his help, I planned an appropriate setting for the pictures. I made a complete set of prints, eleven by fourteen inches, and mounted them—about a hundred in color and black-and-white—in a large white-leather album. These were the pictures that

The sculptor, Giacomo Manzu, works on a head of the Pope.

now appear in this volume. In the name of Archbishop Dearden and myself, this album was sent directly to the Holy Father.

One day the Archbishop called me to his office.

"The Holy Father liked your photographs," he told me. Opening an envelope, he took out a photostatic copy of one of my pictures. "He has asked if you will make fifty copies for him."

This was an honor beyond anything I had hoped for. I made the fifty prints and took them to the Archbishop to be sent to the Pope, and several weeks later I had a magnificent reward. Back to me came one of my prints, autographed by the Holy Father and embossed with his seal.

This is the story of how this book came to be. In the following pages, in words,

The Pope and his unfinished portrait in clay.

and especially in pictures, I have tried to share with my readers the great adventure I had in recording one of the momentous events in modern history, the making of Pope John XXIII.

— Tony Spina

Pope John was a willing listener as Tony Spina explained the techniques of the photographer's art.

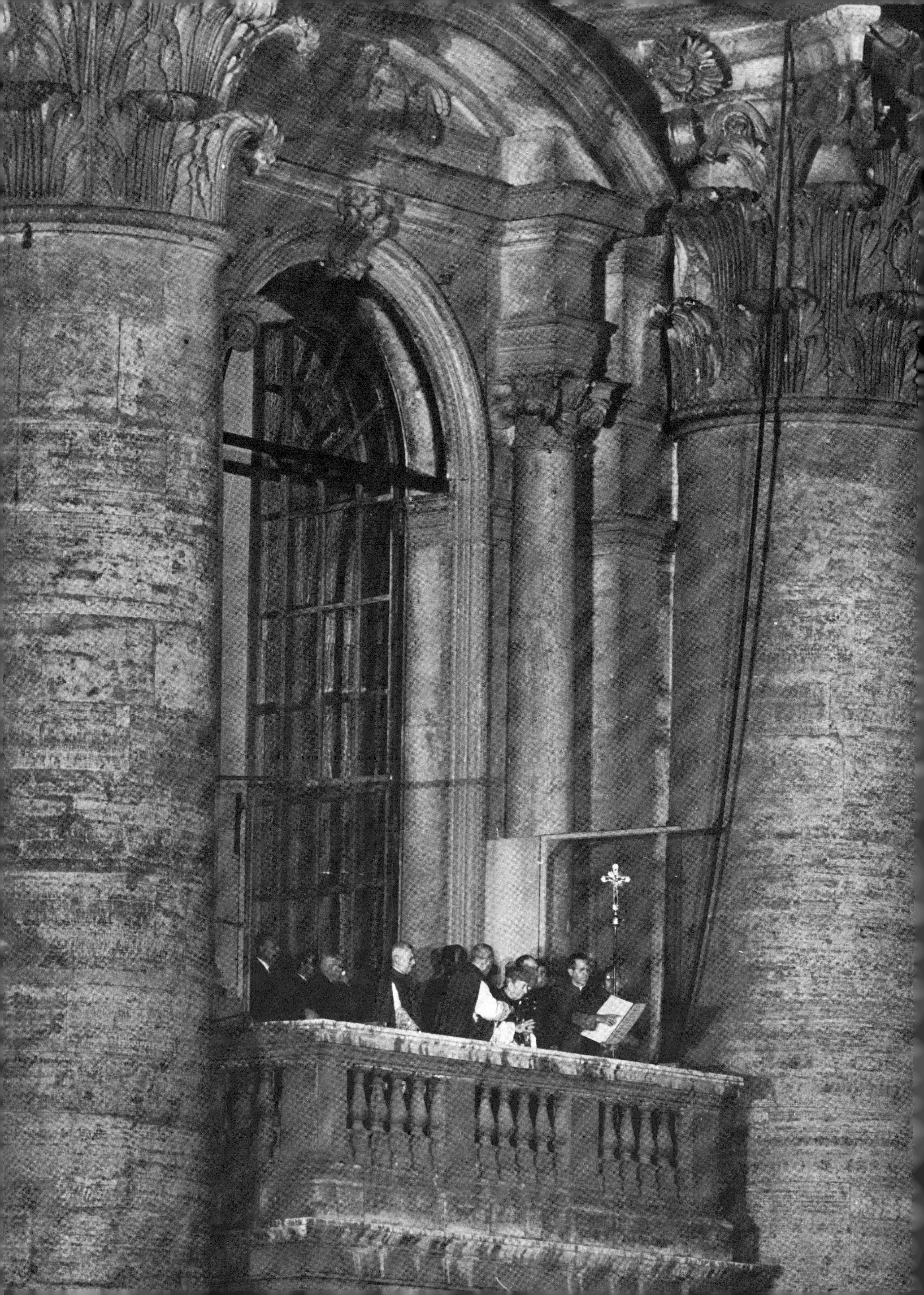

The Election of the Pope

"Habemus Papam."

"We have a Pope." With these words, spoken from the balcony of St. Peter's Basilica at 6:02 P.M. on October 28, 1958, Cardinal Canali announced to the waiting world and to the quarter of a million people who had gathered in St. Peter's Square that a successor to Pope Pius XII had been elected. To the cheering mass he announced that Angelo Giuseppe Roncalli had been elected by the conclave of cardinals and had chosen to be called Pope John XXIII, the 262nd Pope of the Catholic Church, inheritor of the primacy of St. Peter.

The Papal flag was draped over the railing of the balcony to signify the end of the interregnum, that period when the Church was briefly without a head. The Papal troops were drawn up on the steps, and all was ready for the first public appearance of the new Pontiff.

At 6:16 P.M. a momentary hush fell over the square, as Pope John appeared on the balcony. He held his hands outstretched and he pronounced the ancient benediction.

"Urbi et orbi"—"the city and the world"—a legacy from the days when the civilized world was made up of the city of Rome and the world outside.

Then the new Pope left the balcony to the cheers of the huddled mass in the Square, cheers of "long live the Pope," and a new period in the history of the Church had begun. Long after the Pope had left the balcony crowds continued to mill about in the square, caught up in the excitement of this autumn evening. For this evening marked the end of a two day vigil that had begun on Sunday afternoon, when the crowds first started to assemble in St. Peter's Square.

The interregnum had been short. It was only nineteen days since the saintly Pope Pius XII had died at Castel Gandolfo, the Papal summer residence. For three days the body of Eugenio Pacelli had lain in state under the great dome of St. Peter's and thousands had come to pay their last respects to the remains of the Pope who had reigned through the most turbulent two decades in the history of the world.

From this balcony Cardinal Canali announced to the crowd in the square that a new Pope had been elected.

Long ago the Church had recognized the dangers inherent in a long interregnum. Almost immediately the call went out to the cardinals of the Church scattered throughout the world for the conclave that would choose a successor Pope, following the custom of centuries, custom that has come down without basic change for seven hundred years.

Now, with the death of Pius XII, the fifty-four princes of the Church were summoned to come to the Vatican from their residences all over the world. By Papal rule, the interval between the death of the reigning Pope and the start of the electoral conclave was limited to fifteen days—or at the most eighteen—so the cardinals were required to come to Rome without delay. The conclave would be without two of its members, for Cardinal Mindszenty, Archbishop of Esztergom, was living in political asylum in the American Embassy in Budapest, and Cardinal Stepinac, Archbishop of Zagreb, was living in confinement in a tiny Yugoslav village. A third cardinal, Archbishop Mooney of Detroit, was fated to die just before the official opening of the conclave, so the election would rest with fifty-one electors.

By Sunday, October 26, the assembled cardinals were ready for their balloting. Rome was experiencing an Indian summer that late autumn day, with bright sunshine and a temperature hovering around seventy-five degrees. By mid-morning thousands of Romans and visitors from all over the world had assembled in St. Peter's Square to wait for the column of smoke from a temporary chimney over the Sistine Chapel that would signal success or failure in the first balloting. The conclave was surrounded by the greatest secrecy. Not even the leading newspaper correspondents who had assembled in Rome from all over the world were allowed inside the sealed chamber, and only by the pre-arranged smoke signal would the world know whether or not a new Pope had been elected. A column of white smoke would mean that the Sacred College of Cardinals had elected a new Pope; a column of black smoke would mean that the balloting had been indecisive.

Already vague rumors were adrift that there was wide disagreement among the assembled cardinals, and that there was no candidate with strong enough support to assure election. So the crowd was tense on that first morning of the balloting. It was expected that the first announcement would come at about eleven o'clock, and as the time approached the crowd was restive with anticipation. As eleven o'clock passed without a signal the mood of the waiting throng became apprehensive, and as the minutes dragged slowly by the mood became more and more restive.

It was nearly three-quarters of an hour later that the first wisps of smoke were seen issuing from the chimney. At first the thin column appeared white to the waiting people, and a great shout rose from thousands of throats:

"Viva il Papa"—"long live the Pope!"

But as the column of smoke became stronger it turned black and a stunned silence descended over the square. Disappointed and quiet the throng dispersed, to assemble again in the afternoon for another disappointing signal.

Black smoke: the conclave has failed again to elect a Pope.

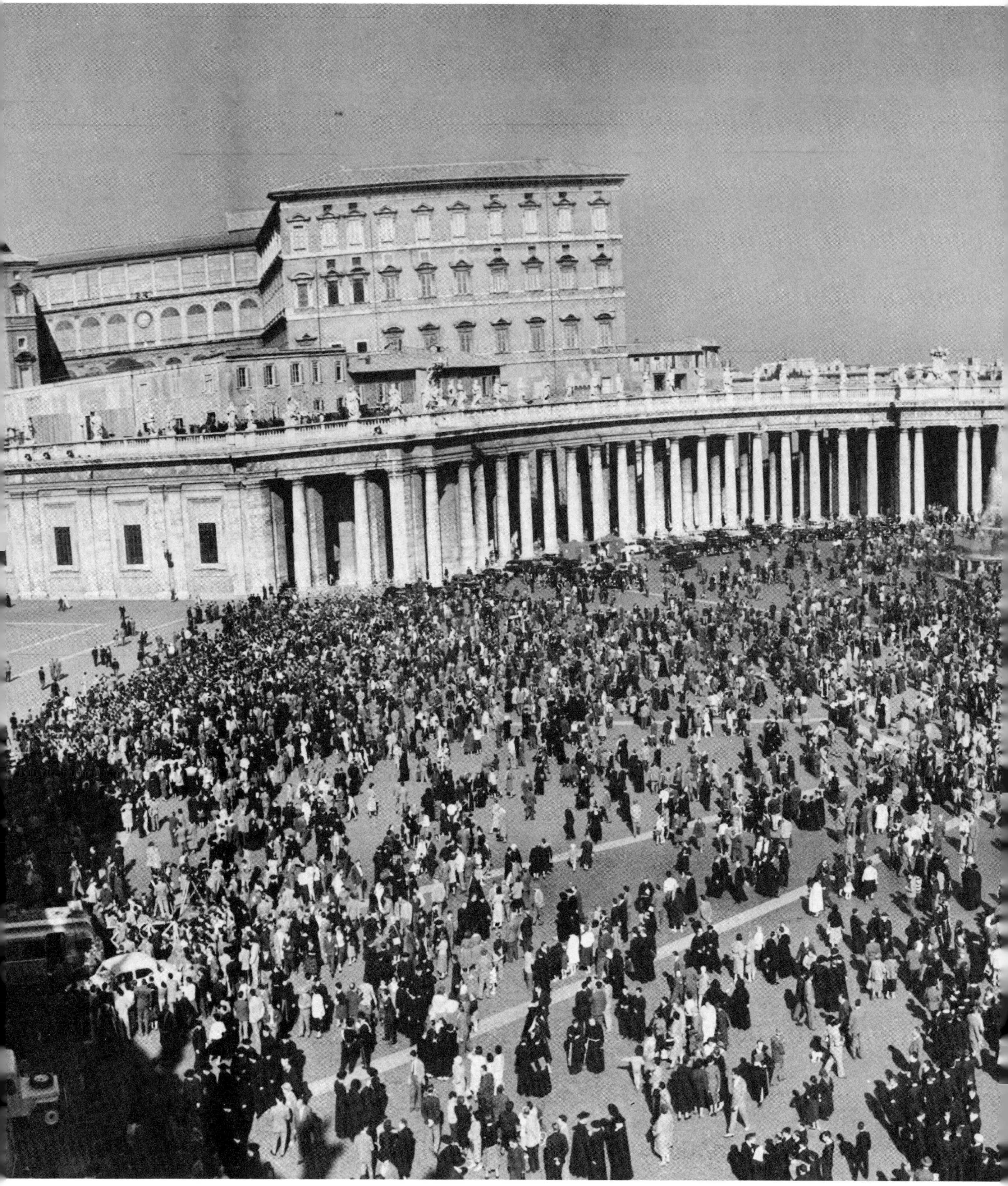

For three days throngs gathered in St. Peter's Square to await smoke signals from the conclave in the Sistine Chapel.

Swarms of starlings darkened the sky over the Sistine Chapel
on the final day of the conclave.

The rooftops of Vatican City.

THE ELECTION OF THE POPE 33

As black signals were issued Monday morning and again Monday evening, the rumors of disagreement in the conclave gained strength. There was talk that the cardinals would have to agree on a compromise Pope, a "caretaker" Pope, and in spite of the intense secrecy surrounding the conclave, the name of Angelo Giuseppe Roncalli, Patriarch of Venice, became prominent in these rumors. It was pointed out that he was popular, that he would be an easy compromise candidate, that he was old—already in his late seventies—an ideal age for a "caretaker" Pope. How these rumors misjudged the strength and influence of the new Pope has been amply proved in the succeeding four years!

On Tuesday morning the smoke signal was again black, indicating the tense situation inside the sealed chamber where the electors were locked in ballot after ballot.

By four o'clock Tuesday afternoon the square was thick with massed humanity. There was a tense feeling that this time the signal would be affirmative. Suddenly the sky over the square was thick with the flight of thousands of starlings, dark over

White smoke from the chimney erected over the Sistine Chapel
signaled the election of Pope John XXIII.

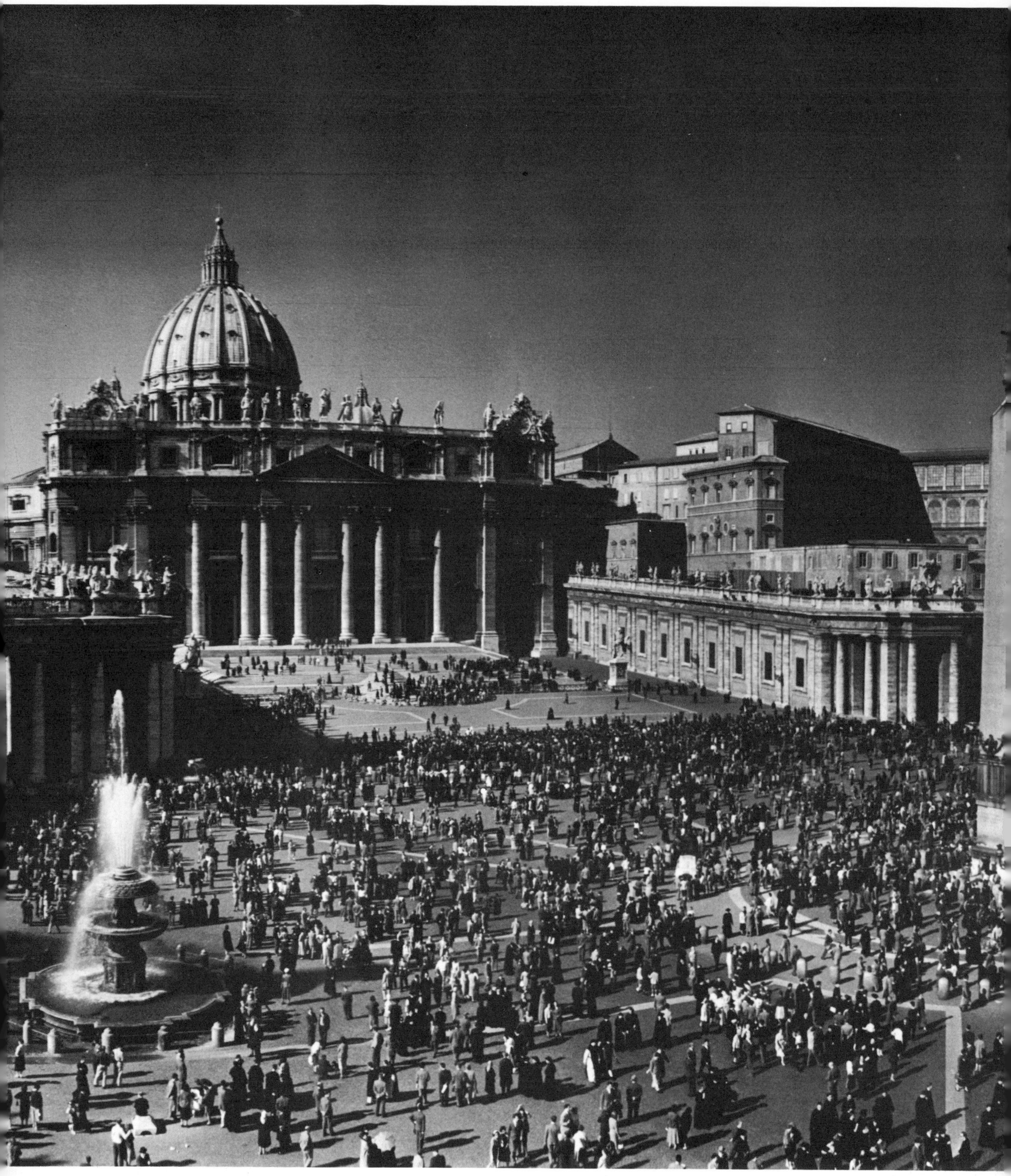

St. Peter's: the crowd gathers for news of the conclave.

St. Peter's Basilica and the Sistine Chapel. For more than a half hour the birds fluttered over the square, like a happy omen.

By five o'clock all eyes were turned toward the chimney over the Sistine Chapel, and at 5:07 exactly the column of smoke fluttered upward. This time there was no mistaking the thick white column, and a happy roar rose over the square. The news went out to the Romans and to the waiting world over the Vatican radio, and in a matter of minutes thousands of people converged on the square to join the thousands already waiting. By six o'clock more than two hundred fifty thousand jammed the square, to hear the momentous announcement and see the first public appearance of the new Pope.

Who was this new Pope, this simple man who had chosen to be known by the Biblical name of John? A long and honored career in the Church had been the testing ground for his elevation to the supreme position, and to his co-workers in the Church he was well known, loved and revered. But to the world outside the Vatican he was little known, and the world would judge him by his words and his deeds. If his predecessor, Pius XII, was a man of intellect, John XXIII is a man of heart.

"From the beginning of my clerical life," he has said, "I aspired only to become a country priest in my diocese. But Providence has wished to send me along other paths." Protesting his unworthiness for this highest post, he has by his deeds proved himself most worthy. He is a "Pope of the people." Far from accepting the passive role of a "caretaker" Pope, he has proved that his character will impress itself upon our age in a manner that few could have foreseen four years ago; his is likely to be one of the notable reigns in the history of the Papacy.

Several contemporary estimates of the Pontiff's character sum up Pope John as his co-workers knew him before he was elevated to the Papacy. Cardinal Montini, Archbishop of Milan, at that time Pro-Secretary of State in the Vatican, was quoted by a newspaper correspondent:

"He is a most lovable person, and it is owing to his natural goodness of soul that a large part of his success as a diplomat is due. When he went to France as nuncio toward the end of 1944, the situation was very uncertain with regard to a large part of the episcopate. It was thanks to the apostolic nuncio that many questions could immediately be answered and that the appointments of bishops could be agreed upon with mutual satisfaction. The new Pontiff is a person of great culture. He loves study, especially history. He is an able conversationalist, is full of a Manzonian sense of humor, and an agreeable story teller who loves a good story. As a confirmation of the sympathy he won for himself in France, it is enough to recall that when ex-President Auriol came to Italy recently, he could not pass up making a trip to see the Patriarch of Venice, Roncalli. The new Pope has the tastes of a humanist and is very keenly interested in art."

Archbishop Urbani of Verona, now the Cardinal Archbishop of Venice, remembers that "the Patriarch was young in temperament, energy, ideas, programs. He knew how to win the sympathy, esteem and affection, the admiration of all, clergy and people. It was almost second nature for him to be simple, frank and amiable. Anyone dealing with him, even with regard to the most complicated matters, was impressed by his ability to smooth difficulties and reduce matters to their essentials. He was quick to find the most suitable and proper solutions. No one ever remembers having seen him angry, no one has ever heard in his voice a tone of irritation or bad humor.

"The constant serenity of spirit, based upon a happy temperament and an inclination toward optimism, appears to one who has known him for a long time to be the fruit of long training in the virtues, the result of interior discipline, the fortunate meeting of a lively intelligence with an ardent heart, tenacious will and balanced character. His evident love for his fellow men and a soul endowed with an appreciation of art, his innate tact and courtesy, his refined nature, these are the qualities which have won him the hearts of all who came into contact with him."

This was the man who could say humbly, after his elevation, when the assembled cardinals knelt before him, "Please forgive me, I am not accustomed to being a Pope." As a man speaks, so he is, and Pope John has perhaps best summed himself up in his brief Coronation Address, on November 4, 1958:

"We greet with a father's affection the cardinals, archbishops, and bishops of the Holy Roman Church who are present either in person or in spirit at these sacred rites in which We, though unworthy, are solemnly entering upon the office of the Supreme Pontiff; and We greet all of you, Our dear children among all the classes of men throughout the world, who are troubled by the cares and anxieties of this present life but are mindful nonetheless of those eternal goods which merit particular attention.

"We are assembled before a great monument to the Prince of Apostles. His august office has been entrusted to Us as his Successor. At this memorable moment We seem to hear the voice of Peter coming to Us across the centuries; We seem to hear the voices of those two Johns, brethren of Our Lord, whose dear and honored name We have chosen to bear.

"In these days that are so full of strange happenings and of anxieties, We have received the congratulations of a great number of men. We are consoled by the expressions of joy with which Our elevation to the Pontificate has been hailed. But on the other hand We are troubled by the great variety of complex tasks that have been placed upon Our shoulders. We refer to tasks which have been described to Us in various ways, set forth by many men in many ways—within certain definite limits—according to their own personal inclinations, practical experience, and the particular perspectives from which they view the life of individuals or society. Some

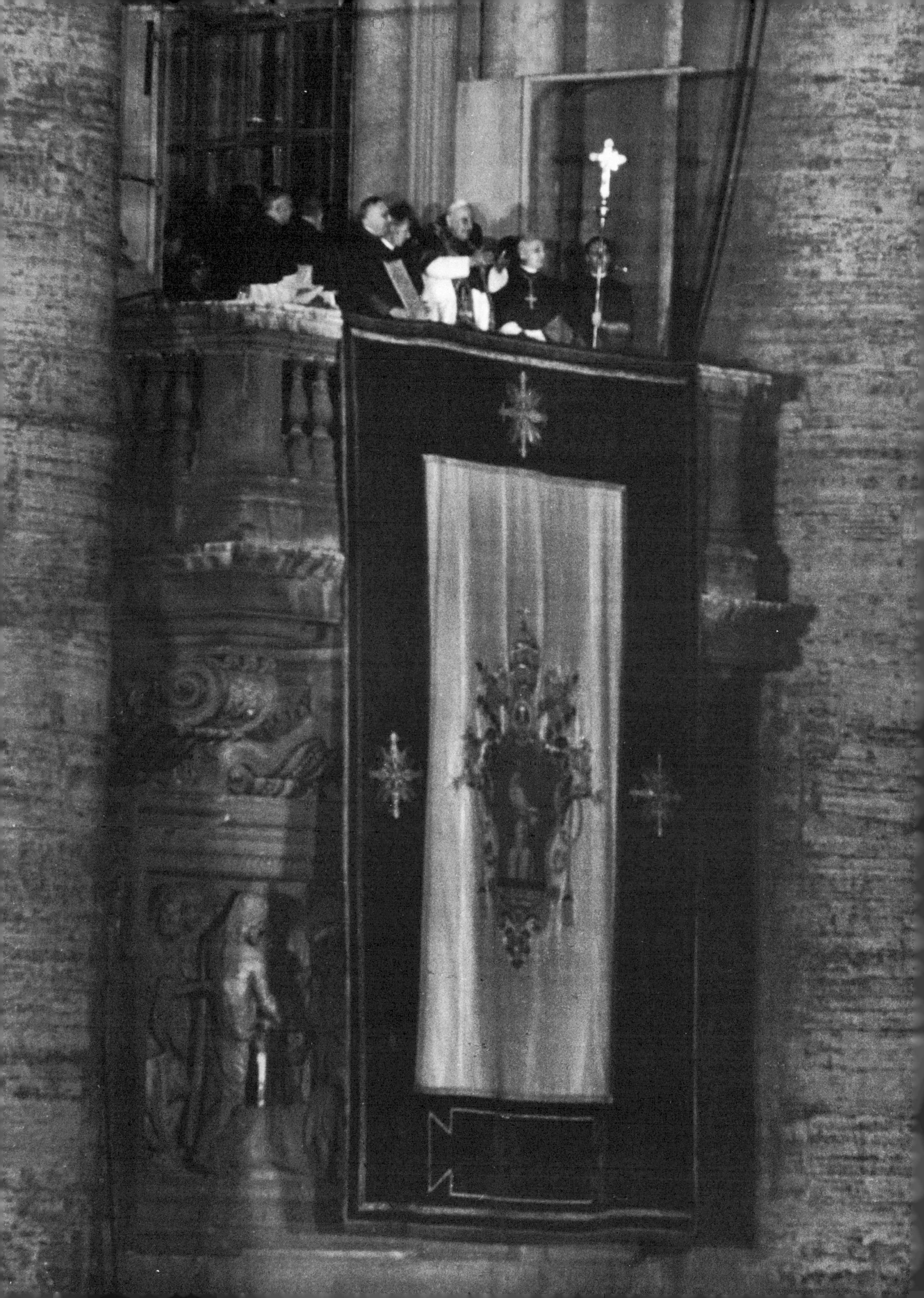

believe the Pope should busy himself in guiding the affairs of nations, that he should be a seasoned diplomat or universal genius, that he should be wise in directing the day-by-day life of man, or that he should be the sort of Pope whose spirit embraces all the advances of this modern age without exception.

"But, Venerable Brothers and beloved sons, they are not on the right track, since they fashion an image of the Supreme Pontiff which is not fully consistent with sound thinking or the purpose of this office.

"For a new Pontiff in the trials of this life is like the son of the Patriarch Jacob, who welcomed his suffering brothers and showed his love and compassion for them, saying "I am Joseph . . . your brother." (Gen. 45,4) By this We mean that a new Pontiff embodies that clear image set forth in the Gospel when St. John describes the good shepherd in the Savior's own words. (cf. John 10, 1-21) No one can enter the sheepfold of Jesus Christ except under the guidance of the Supreme Pontiff. Only when men are in union with him can they safely attain salvation, since the Roman Pontiff is the Vicar of Christ and represents Him on earth. How fine it is to bear in mind this picture of the good shepherd which the Gospel narrative sets out in such exquisite and attractive terms!

"Venerable Brothers and beloved sons, the Roman Pontiffs through the ages, and particularly Our Predecessor Pius XII, have issued warnings on this matter and We now do the same. We assert vigorously and sincerely that it is Our particular intention to be the shepherd, the pastor, of the whole flock. All other human gifts and accomplishments—learning, practical experience, diplomatic finesse—can broaden and enrich pastoral work, but they can not replace it.

"A special place must be given the zeal and concern of the good shepherd who is ready for the most difficult tasks, who is outstanding for his prudence, uprightness and steadfastness, who does not fear danger. 'The good shepherd gives his life for his sheep. (John 10, 11) With what beauty is the Church of Christ. 'the sheepfold,' (ib. 10, 1) resplendent! The shepherd 'goes before the sheep' (cf. ib. 10, 4) and they all follow him. To defend them he does not fear to ward off the attacks of the wolf.

"And then the mind turns to even deeper thoughts: 'Other sheep I have that are not of this fold. Them also must I bring, and they shall hear my voice, and there shall be one fold and one shepherd.' (ib. 10, 16) These words sum up the hope and the splendor of all missionary work. This activity is certainly the first concern of the Roman Pontiff, though not the only one, for even of itself it involves many other cares that are no less important."

The first public appearance of Pope John XXIII just after the announcement of his election.

The Papal banner bears the coat-of-arms of Pius XII.

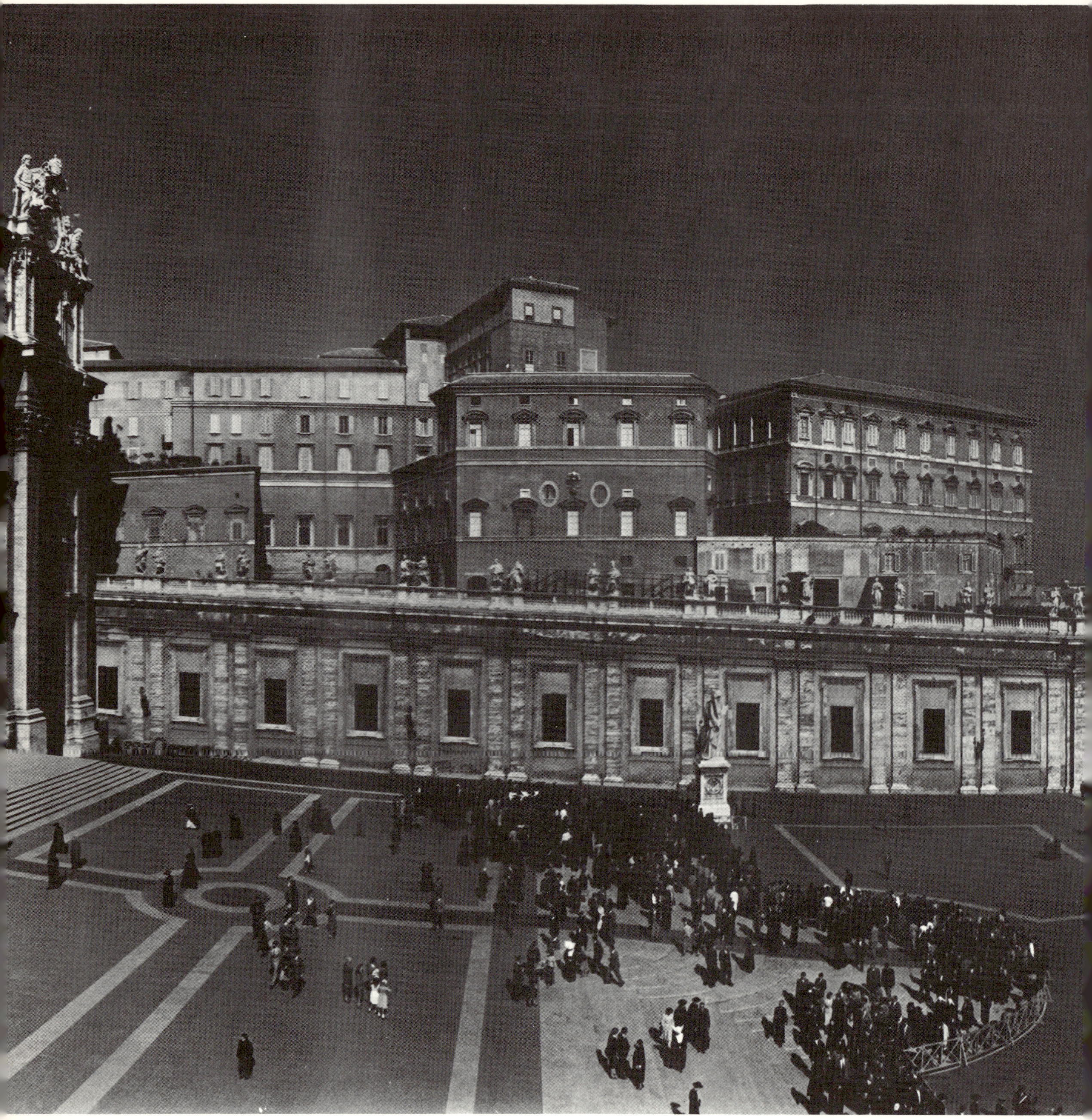

A quarter of a million people crowded St. Peter's Square on the evening of
October 28, 1958, when the announcement was made of the election
of a new Pope.

The Development of the Papacy

In our time the election of a new Pope has achieved universal significance. Even though the Church of Rome neither seeks nor asserts temporal power outside the Vatican State, nevertheless its authority and influence transcend national boundaries. The Pope today holds the most powerful office in the entire history of Western civilization; his spiritual leadership of more than five hundred million humans is unquestioned, and his voice in world affairs is heard with respect by the heads of state throughout the world.

When a sorrowing world learned of the death of Pope Pius XII in 1958, no event anywhere in the world transcended in importance and interest the meeting of the cardinals in Rome to elect his successor. News services carried reports hour by hour; no national election anywhere could have had the impact of the balloting that was under way in the sealed chamber in the Vatican.

It was not always so. The influence and power of the Papacy have grown and developed slowly and painfully through the centuries, through the early history of the Church, when Popes, along with their faithful followers, were subject to martyrdom in their struggle to keep alive and to spread the new faith proclaimed by Jesus Christ and His Disciples; through the Dark Ages, when the Church alone kept alive the faint lamp of learning; through the great schism, when the Church broke apart and formed two dissident units; through the struggle with the protestant dissenters, to its modern position of unquestioned leadership of those who have adhered to the Catholic faith. The Papacy has suffered persecution and death, armed assault and captivity—every indignity known to man—but it has emerged in our time as the oldest and strongest institution in the annals of Western man. Today the Pope carries the titles of "Bishop of Rome, Vicar of Jesus Christ, Succesor of the Prince of Apostles, Supreme Pontiff of the Universal Church, Patriarch of the West, Primate of Italy, Archbishop and Metropolitan of the Roman Province, Sovereign of the State of the City of the Vatican." These are not empty panegyrics. Each of these great titles represents a phase of Papal authority earned, often bitterly, and solidified through twenty centuries of growth.

THE DEVELOPMENT OF THE PAPACY

The Papacy is a unique office and an awesome responsibility. It demands and exhausts the full strength of those who hold it. The Pope must be exemplary in character; every detail of his life must be above the slightest reproach. He must surrender almost every reserve of privacy; he must be devoted day and night, in his person and in his spiritual being, to his office. He is charged with the political responsibility for the conduct of his office and of the Vatican State, yet he must be above politics. He can not avoid the temporal implications in the daily lives of his half-billion adherents; yet he must not deviate even in the most trying circumstances from spiritual righteousness. He can not, like his contemporary temporal heads of state, seek expedient solutions to immediate problems, for he must remain always the interpreter of the Kingdom of Heaven to his beseeching, questioning, demanding children.

Never, in the history of the world, has so much attention been focused on the Pope. His slightest utterance, not only on matters of Church doctrine, but upon any world problem, commands the widest attention. He lives constantly in the spotlight, and he must choose with the greatest care every word he speaks or writes, for it will be subjected to the most careful scrutiny and analysis. And rightly so, for the fate of the Western world is very much bound up with the conduct of Church affairs.

The history of the Church has in many periods been a stormy one, but through its trials and tribulations the present solid foundation of Papal authority has been developed. For the first two centuries after the ascension of our Saviour, Christianity gained strength and followers slowly and painfully, defying the Roman authority; during some periods in these centuries, the Christians actually carried on their meetings underground, utilizing the catacombs—underground burial places—for their religious services. By the third century, Christianity had established itself as a strong force, but still against the opposition of Roman authority; its status at any time was determined largely by the personal inclinations of the emperor in power at the moment.

The first half of the third century brought a temporary peace to the Church, but in 249 Decius succeeded to the imperial power, and he embarked upon a cruel and ruthless campaign to destroy Christianity. By edict he forbade the practice of Christianity and decreed that all Christians were to give tangible evidence of their abandonment of their religion. Refusal to do so was made the grounds for torture and even death. Among the first Christians to suffer martyrdom under this edict was the reigning Pope, Fabian, who is numbered among the saints.

The latter half of the third century saw the beginnings of the dissension that was to erupt at intervals from that time on. Doctrinal controversies and the brief appearance of an antipope foreshadowed the more serious dissensions of future centuries, but the Popes were able to consolidate their position and by the end of the century the supremacy of the Papacy in Church matters had become secure.

The early years of the fourth century saw a resurgence of Christian persecution. The Emperor Diocletian ordered the confiscation of Church property and the destruction of Christian books. Christians were ordered to deny their faith or suffer martyrdom, and again the Pope, Marcellinus, was a victim of this persecution, which did not officially cease until the cruel and infamous Emperor Galerian, repenting of his acts when he became ill, issued a decree of toleration in 311.

The next year saw the historic turning point in the development of the Church. The Emperor Constantine, not himself a Christian, nevertheless proclaimed that he had seen the cross in a vision as his sign of victory. In gratitude for the victory which did indeed come to him, he issued his famous decree of toleration which was to set the Christians free.

It was in the rule of Constantine also that the first of the ecumenical, or worldwide, councils was called to settle a matter of doctrinal controversy. The Council of Nicaea was of greatest importance to the future of the Church, because it established a pattern for the orderly development of doctrinal policy that has been followed ever since. Through discussion and decisions taken in ecumenical council, rules of doctrinal procedure are set forth that are infallible and may thenceforth not be questioned. In all, twenty councils have been convened which the Church recognizes as ecumenical, the twentieth having been convened by Pope Pius IX in 1869. The announcement by Pope John XXIII of the convening of an ecumenical council has been met with worldwide interest, and as this book was on press the council, the first in nearly a century, was being convened.

The Council of Nicaea became necessary because of the heretical teaching of the priest Arius of Alexandria. Arius had denied the divinity of Jesus Christ, and had gathered a large following on this point of doctrinal deviation. The Emperor Constantine himself was present when the Council was convened at Nicaea, and the outcome was a statement of doctrinal policy to which the Church has since remained firmly committed, the Nicene Creed, which proclaims that Jesus Christ is "true God of true God, consubstantial with the Father."

In the eleventh century there occurred the first general disruption in the unity of the Christian Church. There can be no doubt that reform within the Church was long overdue. Christianity had become the official state religion throughout the Western world, and in many places churchmen exercised or fought for temporal power. Church offices and favors were openly bought and sold, and even the Papacy was not immune to the corruption which had become general. When the Eastern Schism finally became a fact in 1054, it was not over any deep seated difference in religious belief or doctrine, but simply over the recognition of the nature of the primacy of the Pope. While this is not the place for an extended discussion of the history of the Church, it should be noted that the "Orthodox" Church is not in fact a single Church, but a group of no less than seventeen autonomous churches, each with its own head, or patriarch. All differ from the Roman Catholic Church in their refusal to recognize the primacy of the Pope as the head of the Christian Church. While there is some variation among the Orthodox Churches, in general they adhere closely to Catholic doctrine in other respects and feel themselves bound by the first seven of the ecumenical councils.

By the time of the Eastern Schism, the Church had already begun to set its own house in order. The reform of the corrupt Church may be said to have begun with the founding of a Benedictine Monastery at Cluny, France, in an attempt to restore the primitive simplicity and high moral tone of the Christian beginnings. The reform movement spread rapidly, and reached its climax in 1059 when, by the decree of the Synod of the Lateran, the College of Cardinals was established as a permanent body to govern the Church and to elect the Popes. In spite of recurring periods of turbulence and dissension, the corruption of the Dark Ages had been stemmed, never to recur. Today the College of Cardinals has unrivalled authority and prestige as the governing advisory body of the Church.

The Medieval period was notable for two great movements. The first was the series of Crusades, sponsored by the Papacy, the announced purpose of which was to wrest the Holy Land from the control of Islam. The Crusades, which drained Europe physically and emotionally for more than two centuries, represented a truly great epic in the history of mankind. Entire populations were inspired to heroism and sacrifice; Europe was inflamed, with religious fervor at a high pitch. Regardless of the motives that might have moved the Popes and the leaders of the various expeditions, to the people who participated the Crusades were a great adventure, and the returning Crusaders brought from the East the first faint stirrings of the coming Renaissance.

The second great movement of the Middle Ages was the intermittent struggle between the clergy and the lay authority for dominance. It makes little difference whether we regard this as a struggle of the Church for temporal power, or an attempt by the heads of state to control the Church; the end result was the great series of Protestant Revolutions that severed the loyalty to the Catholic Church in much of western Europe.

The corruption of the Church by its highest authorities had become a universal scandal, and all those who loved truth, goodness and righteousness were deeply concerned. Both within the Church and without men were aghast at the sale of Church offices, marriage and immorality of the clergy, political conspiracy and the open disregard of the very ethical foundations of religion. For more than a century strong efforts had been made to reform the Church from within, with the decree of 1059 as a major result. The times called for a great man, and fortunately for the Church a great man came forward to answer that need.

By the time Gregory VII ascended to the Papacy 1073, he had already proved himself able, vigorous, honest, irreproachable. A man of humble beginnings, his name was Hildebrand (thus the term Hildebrandine reforms, for which his reign was noted). He became a Benedictine and rose through successive appointments to a high position in the Church hierarchy. In the twelve years of his reign, he compiled a notable record as a reformer, ending the corrupt practices of the clergy, which reached even up to the Papacy. Specifically he forbade marriage of the clergy, sale of Church offices, and investiture of Church officers by lay authorities. No one did so much to restore the waning prestige of the Church in his time as did Gregory

VII, and for his glorious services to the Church and his holy life he was canonized.

With the death of Gregory VII, the struggle between Church and State broke out with renewed fury throughout Europe. The question of lay investiture, by which heads of state conferred Church offices as political favors, had been challenged forthrightly by the Pope, and in France, Germany and England the struggle for dominance went on with increased vigor and bloodshed. In England Henry II appointed as Archbishop of Canterbury and head of the Church his chancellor and friend Thomas à Becket, and when Becket fought Henry's interference in the affairs of the Church, the King had his friend murdered brutally within the sanctuary of the cathedral itself.

The French kings opposed the Papacy tenaciously, and in 1309, King Philip IV "captured" the Papacy and established the Popes at Avignon, in Southern France, where the seat of the Church remained in "captivity" until 1378. Even after the return of the Popes to Rome, the incident was not closed, and for the next forty years, the years of the "Great Schism," the Popes at Rome had rival "antipopes" sitting at Avignon.

With the coming of the Renaissance in Rome, the demand for Church reform grew more insistent. The Popes were more concerned with art and literature than they were with religion. Insistent calls for Church reform became increasingly frequent in the fifteenth century, and by the time Pope Paul III had convened the most important of all ecumenical councils in Trent in 1545, the breach had already opened too wide to mend. In 1517, after appeals to Rome had failed, Martin Luther issued his ninety-five theses, and it was too late to erase the errors of the past.

The Council of Trent was the supreme effort of the Papacy to stem the tide of revolution. Its accomplishments were great, and had it come two centuries earlier, it might have altered the course of history. In some twenty-five sessions convened over a period of eighteen years, the Council redefined many areas of Catholic doctrine in language and purpose so clear that it has served to guide the Church for the last four centuries. Only one other ecumenical council has been convened in the interval, the Vatican Council, which in 1870 set forth the principle of Papal infallibility and defined the supreme authority of the Pope in modern times.

But the revolution was in full swing. In Germany, Switzerland, the Low Countries, in Poland, France, and Scotland, dissident churchmen were heeding the rebellion of Luther and Calvin, and new non-Catholic congregations were coming into being, each with its splinter dissensions on matters of doctrine or ritual. In England, Henry VIII saw political and personal advantage in the revolution, and swept away the accumulated traditions of centuries in a moment. Here the dissension was not one of doctrine, but of personal convenience, but no matter, the end result was the same: in spite of two centuries of bitter and often bloody fighting, the Roman Catholic Church had lost England.

Today the Roman Catholic Church can with some justice lay claim to being the only Church in the world that practices the Christian faith as it was laid down by our Savior and as it is set forth in the Apostles' Creed. All other branches of Christianity deviate in some degree: the Orthodox churches only in their denial of the primacy of the Pope, the Protestant churches in slight or major matters of doctrine.

The Catholic Church stands today as the strongest institution in the modern world and the most widespread in area and influence. It holds spiritual domination over nearly five hundred fifty million human beings, who look to the Vatican for guidance, for hope, for faith.

Street scene: a typical morning in Vatican City.

The State of the City of the Vatican

"Thou art Peter and upon this rock I will build my Church and to thee I will give the keys of the kingdom of heaven."

These words, engraved in black mosaic against a gold background in the frieze high up in the dome of St. Peter's, represent and mark the very heart of the Catholic Church. For here, on the very spot where the remains of St. Peter lie, the lifebeat of the Church has its being, and from here the lifeblood of the Church circulates throughout the Christian world.

St. Peter's, standing in its magnificent square, is the center of the State of the City of the Vatican, the world's smallest independent state. It is also one of the newest, having been created only a generation ago by the Lateran Treaty between the Church and the Italian government in the Pontificate of Pius XI.

For more than a thousand years the Popes had reigned as temporal rulers over a large part of what is now Italy. In 756 Pepin, King of the Franks, ceded to Pope Stephen a belt of land across central Italy, which remained for eleven centuries the "Papal States," administered by the government of the Church. It was not until 1870, when Garibaldi accomplished the unification of modern Italy, that the Papal States ceased to be and the Popes became solely spiritual rulers.

For two generations an uneasy peace existed between the Papacy and the Italian government. The Vatican existed as an island in the troubled sea of Italian politics, the Popes voluntary prisoners within the Vatican. The negotiation of the Lateran Treaty ended this difficult situation and gave the Vatican the free and independent position it now holds. Under the terms of the treaty the Vatican's right to political independence is fully recognized, including the right of self-government, coinage, postal system, maintenance of its army, and fixed boundaries. The relations between the Vatican and the Italian government were defined, and the Italian government paid an indemnity of $92,000,000 for the seizure of the Papal States six decades previously.

The Vatican State comprises about 108 acres, nearly half consisting of beautiful gardens. It has a permanent population of about one thousand, of which about ninety per cent are men. It issues its own coinage and its own postage stamps, which are beautifully designed and much prized by collectors. It maintains its own tiny army, governs its own territory of about one-sixth of a square mile, and even operates a tiny railroad by which supplies are brought in from Rome twice weekly over its half mile of track. Vatican employees are paid salaries which, by Italian standards, are quite comfortable and are entirely tax-free. (As one of his official acts, Pope John authorized an "across-the-board" pay increase for all Vatican employees.)

To support the needs of the tiny state, the Vatican has a healthy financial program. "Peter's Pence," which originated as a penny-per-year collection from each family in the Medieval period, has its continuation in the annual collection in Catholic parishes throughout the world today. The Vatican has benefited from bequests of wealthy individuals, and derives substantial income from the sale of postage stamps to collectors, as well as from the sale of reproductions of paintings and other works of art. It has astutely invested the reparations payment received under the terms of the Lateran Treaty throughout the world.

The "main street" of Vatican City, the Way of the Pilgrim, boasts several shops,

Basilica of St. Peter, viewed early on an autumn evening in 1958.

including a well stocked pharmacy. On a side street are to be found a baker's shop and a grocery. From the Papal Estate at Castel Gandolfo come supplies of fresh fruits, vegetables, and meats, and the daily ration per citizen of one-quarter liter of red or white wine.

The Vatican's daily newspaper, the famous *Osservatore Romano,* has a circulation and influence far beyond the borders of the state, and the official radio station has recently added the most modern television broadcasting equipment. The Vatican can boast of the lowest crime rate of any state in recorded history, with an average of one crime per year; its tiny prison finds itself with its three cells unoccupied most of the time.

Under the aegis of the Vatican, there are some thirty-five colleges, including three Papal Universities in Rome. The North American College, in which students from the United States are resident, looks down from the famous Janiculum Hill. The Papal Universities offer a graduate curriculum. They are the Gregorian University, a Jesuit school with more than two thousand students from countries throughout the world; the Collegium Angelicum, a Dominican school specializing in philosophy and theology, and the Collegium Antonianum, the Franciscan school

Basilica of St. Peter, seen through the massive colonnades.

A Swiss guard on sentry duty.

devoted to pedagogy and missionary training. Other schools specialize in Bible study, canon law, and other subjects related to Church history and practice.

The Vatican "armies" are small in numbers, outfitted in uniforms that date to the Renaissance, and are totally lacking in intercontinental ballistic missiles and other modern armament. But they are symbolic of the independence of the Vatican and men have in the past vied for the honor of serving in them. They comprise four units, with a total strength of about three hundred.

The Noble Guard is the elite of the Papal Armies. This select unit, commanded traditionally by a Roman prince, draws its complement from the Catholic nobility of Italy. Its sole function is to serve as an honorary guard for the person of the Pope. The Palatine Guard comprises about eighty men who serve on guard duty in the Papal antechambers and during the Pope's appearances in St. Peter's and the Sistine Chapel. The Papal Gendarmes are the working policemen of the Vatican State. This unit of three officers and one hundred men serves the Vatican in all the usual guard duties, and is drawn from Italian middle class families.

The oldest, most famous, and most colorful of the Vatican armies is the Swiss Guard. This unit was organized first in 1505, to serve as a body guard for Pope Julius II, and except for brief interruptions, it has served all of the Popes since that time. This force is recruited entirely from unmarried Swiss Catholics, eighteen to twenty-five years old, at least five feet eight inches in height, and of good physical appearance. They stand sentry duty, bearing sixteenth century halberds and wearing colorful Renaissance uniforms of bright blue and orange. (Legend—if not history—credits the inspiration for the uniform design to Michelangelo.)

When at full strength, the Swiss Guard consists of ten officers and 127 men. In recent years the Vatican has not been able to recruit sufficient replacements to keep the Swiss Guard at full strength, and the number has fallen below a hundred. In these days of full employment and high salaries, the heavy armor, the strict discipline, and long hours of duty are not appealing to young men.

The Swiss Guard constitute a government unto themselves. They have their own barracks, their own church, even their own cemetery. While no one seriously foresees their usefulness in war, they are issued real rifles with live ammunition, and they spend long hours in rifle drill and practice in modern infantry tactics, preparing for a battle that will never come. It was not always so. In 1527, the Guard stood against German and Spanish troops in defense of Pope Clement VII, killing eight hundred of the enemy. In this action, nearly the entire Guard was wiped out, only twelve men surviving, and on the sixth of May each year, new recruits are inducted into the service in a colorful ceremony which commemorates the little army's proudest moment.

The Vatican is the heart of the Roman Catholic Church, and St. Peter's is its soul. The ground of the Vatican is sacred to Catholics the world over. It has been consecrated with the blood of thousands of Christian martyrs. On the very spot where the tall obelisk stands near the center of the great plaza of St. Peter's Basilica,

Swiss guards stand at attention in the Vatican Palace.

legend says that St. Peter, the first Pope, chosen by Jesus Christ himself, begged to be crucified head downward, because he did not feel himself worthy of being crucified head upright as his Master had been. St. Peter's body lies buried in this ground, and for centuries the tomb has been the object of greatest reverence for the Christian world.

The visitor approaches St. Peter's from the east and enters through the great encompassing arms of the famous Bernini Colonnades. As he enters the plaza, the Piazza San Pietro, he is overwhelmed by the size and grandeur of the scene before him. The plaza stretches before him, a thousand feet in length, three-quarters of that distance in breadth. Here is a great stage for the human drama that has been

A guard poses for Photographer Spina.

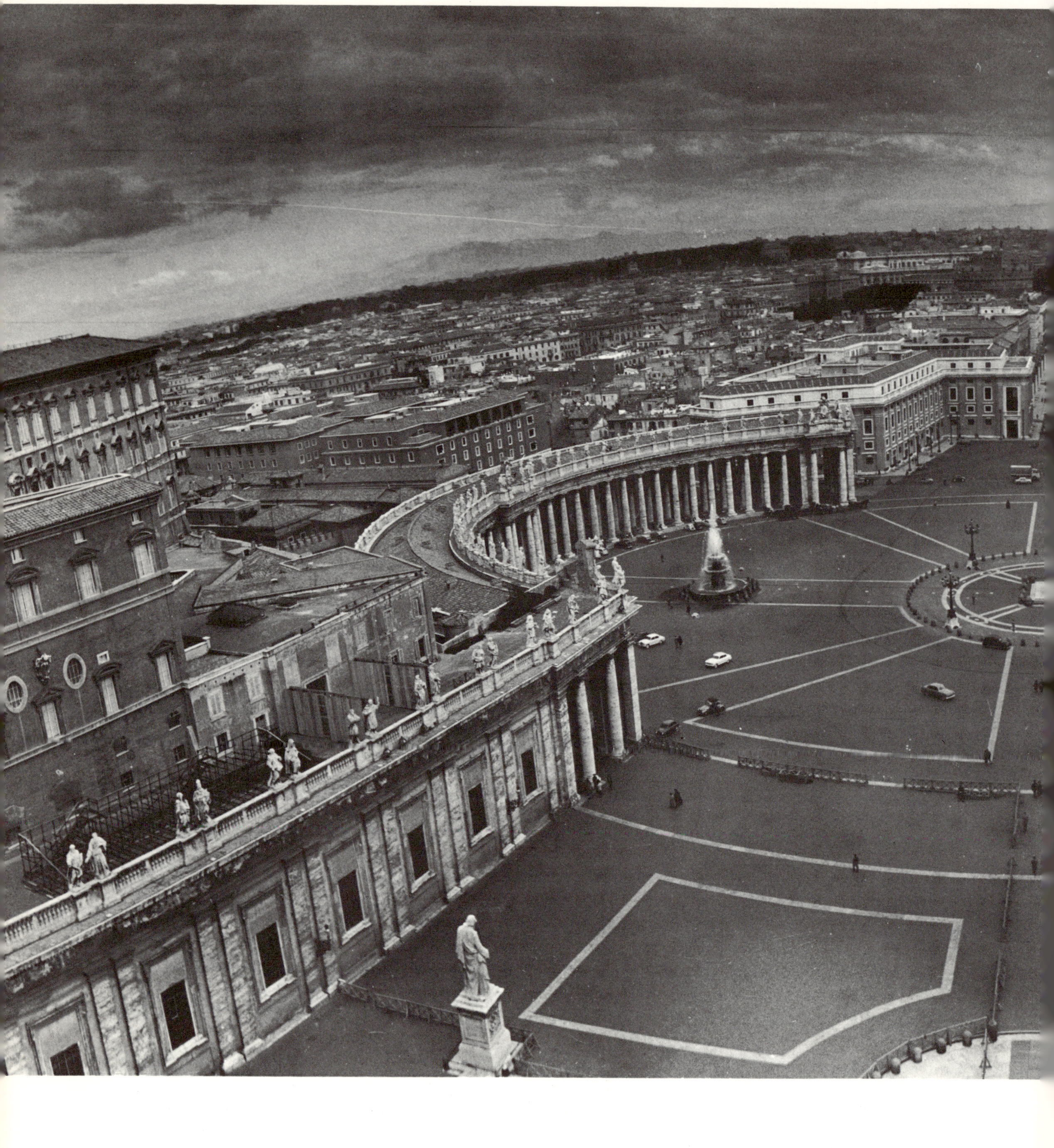

St. Peter's Square, seen from the basilica.

Swiss guards in their colorful medieval uniforms,
said to have been designed by Michelangelo.

enacted over the centuries. Here, on historic occasions, as many as three hundred thousand people have gathered together. The colonnades, with the inner rows placed sixteen feet apart, are symmetrical and beautifully constructed, each consisting of two double rows of travertine marble columns sixty-four feet in height.

Near the center of the enormous square is the giant obelisk which dominates the plaza. It is believed that the obelisk, a great monolith 135 feet in height, was brought from Egypt in the reign of the cruel Emperor Caligula, about 39 A.D. It was erected in the circus, where it was witness to the barbaric bouts of the gladiators, and later to the martyrdom of countless Christians.

Because it was thus associated with the suffering of the early martyrs, Pope Sixtus V in 1586 directed that the obelisk should be moved to the plaza of St. Peter's and

A view over the rooftops to the great central dome of St. Peter's.

ECCE CRVX DOMINI
FVGITE
PARTES ADVERSAE

VICIT LEO
DE TRIBV IVDA

erected there. At its top was placed a great iron cross and inside it a relic of the true cross. On its granite base are inscribed in Latin the words: *Behold the Cross of the Lord; flee thou enemies, the lion of Judah has conquered.* And on the opposite side: *Christ conquers, Christ reigns, Christ rules, may Christ guard this people against all evil.*

The history of St. Peter's itself goes back almost to the beginning of Christianity. It is believed that Pope Anacletus (St. Cletus) in about 80 A.D. built a chapel near the spot where St. Peter lay buried. The construction of the cathedral dates to the reign of Emperor Constantine, under whose rule Christianity won its first real freedom. Constantine, in gratitude for his victories under the sign of the cross, began the construction of St. Peter's Basilica in 326, and it was completed in fourteen years. This structure remained extant for more than eleven centuries.

By the reign of Pope Julius II, the church had fallen into complete disrepair, and it was in the sixteenth century that the present basilica was erected. In all the construction required one hundred twenty years, and some of the greatest artists and architects of Italy's Golden Age had a major part in the construction. The old church was demolished under the direction of the architect Bramante, and his contemporary Raphael was closely associated with the work at this stage.

But foremost of all, St. Peter's is an everlasting tribute to the work of Michelangelo, the greatest architect of them all. He altered the basic plans of Bramante and built the great dome, which towers more than 150 feet over the structure and has a diameter at its base of 138 feet. The mosaics in the dome are one of the great wonders of the modern world and an unforgettable sight to the visitor.

The basilica was planned as a splendid monument to the first Pope, and as a temple that would be a fitting glorification of Christ. It was designed as a Greek cross, with four arms of equal length. But even before its completion in 1590, the original plan had already proved too small, and under the direction of Pope Paul V, the basilica was enlarged by altering the original plan to a Latin cross, with a long extension to one arm and the addition of an elaborate façade. The new plans were prepared by the architect Carlo Maderna, and the alterations were completed in 1612. It was fourteen years later, on November 18, 1626, the thirteenth centenary of the consecration of the original Constantinian Basilica of St. Peter, that Pope Urban VIII presided over ceremonies consecrating the altered basilica.

The vestibule of the basilica is a masterpiece of design and decoration. Its length is 460 feet and the decoration on its vaulted ceiling represents scenes from the lives of the Apostles. Wrought iron gates guard the entrance and on marble slabs on either side are inscribed the names of all the cardinals, archbishops and bishops of the Church who were present at the declaration of the Dogma of the Assumption of the Blessed Virgin.

The great bronze central doors were a part of the old basilica. Executed by Antonio Averulino upon commission by Pope Eugenius IV in the middle of the fifteenth century, the doors are over twenty-five feet in height and weigh more than

This great obelisk was erected in the plaza of St. Peter's in the sixteenth century.

PIO · IX · PONT · MAX ·
QVI · PETRI · ANNOS
IN · PONTIFICATV · ROMANO
VNVS · AEQVAVIT
CLERVS · VATICANVS
SACRAM · ORNAVIT · SEDEM
XVI · KAL · QVINT · A · MDCCCLXXI

Vatican Palace: The Royal Hall.

a thousand pounds. The magnificent reliefs depict our Savior and our Lady and scenes from the lives of St. Peter and St. Paul. St. Peter is shown handing the keys to the kneeling Pope Eugenius IV.

The interior of the basilica is breathtaking in its size. The interior area of St. Peter's is nearly ten acres, including the side chapels and the sacristy, and it is said that one hundred thousand people could be comfortably accommodated within the basilica. The height of the basilica from the ground to the cross atop the dome is 444 feet, and in addition to the great central dome there are ten other

This bronze figure of St. Peter is one of the greatest shrines in the basilica.

CLEMENS·X·PONT·MAX·
ANNO·IVBILEI·MDCLXXV·

Looking upward into the dome of St. Peter's, for a view of one of the priceless mosaics.

domes over the side chapels. Before taking leave of statistics, we should note that St. Peter's has 290 windows, 597 pillars, 44 altars, 131 mosaics and 435 sculptured figures. There is only one painting in the cathedral—the Holy Trinity in the Chapel of the Blessed Sacrament. All of the other views are mosaics, beautifully and colorfully designed.

The main pillars of the basilica contain forty niches, in each of which is a great sculptured figure sixteen feet in height of the founders of the principal orders and congregations. The size and splendor of the buildings are overwhelming as one makes his way along the nave to the Confession which covers the tomb of St. Peter. The balustrade of the Confession is decorated with ninety-five gilt votive lamps which burn day and night. A beautifully wrought trelliswork of bronze encloses a niche over the tomb of the Apostle.

The Papal altar rises above the grave of St. Peter. It is hewn from a single great block of marble, and only the Pope or his appointee may celebrate Mass at this altar. Above the altar is the splendid canopy designed by the sculptor Bernini, surmounted by a cross; the height from the base of the altar to the top of the cross is ninety-three feet. The canopy by Bernini was one of the works of art commissioned by Pope Urban VIII.

he Holy Year Door, opened only during a Jubilee Year.

This magnificent upward panoramic view shows the central altar of St. Peter's with its great canopy by Bernini and the dome.

Among the most ancient art in the basilica is the bronze seated figure of St. Peter which dates from the fourth century and was venerated in the old basilica. The right foot is worn smooth from the kisses of millions of pilgrims. On the feasts of St. Peter and St. Paul and on such important occasions as the coronation of a Pope or the canonization of a saint, this figure is clothed in a cape of gold brocade and crowned with a tiara of precious jewels.

Perhaps the most famous of the chapels of St. Peter's is the Chapel of the Pietà. Many rate this as Michelangelo's greatest work; the "Pietà" was completed when the artist was only twenty-four years old and it is the only one of his extant works which bears his signature. Michelangelo made this famous sculpture for Cardinal Jean de Villiers, the ambassador of King Charles VIII of France. Many critics regard this as a perfect example of the sculptor's art. The Madonna is young, to stress her

This splendid view from the dome of St. Peter's shows the gardens of Vatican City and the residence of the mayor, erected in the Pontificate of Pius XII.

This panoramic view takes in the Papal Altar and dome of St. Peter's, with some of its magnificent works of art.

This view, inside the basilica, looks directly down
on St. Peter's altar from the dome.

ALTARE
PRIVILEGIATVM
PRO
DEFVNCTIS

Hadrian's Tomb and Castel San Angelo

virginity and her imperishable purity. She holds the dead Jesus in her arms; on her face is an expression of profound sorrow and resignation. As this is being written there is some discussion of bringing the famous sculpture to New York for the coming World Fair, but this is not certain, for it is feared that there would be some danger in transporting and erecting the great work.

In the basilica is also the Treasury, a small museum which houses objects of religious art and reliquaries of incredible value. Crucifixes and monstrances of plat-

The Pietà, Michelangelo's masterwork.

inum, ember, rock crystal, Japanese enamel and gold, studded with precious jewels, may be seen here, and here is housed the precious tiara which is placed on special occasions on the head of St. Peter. The relics of our Savior and the Apostles lend special significance to the Mass and to the Catholic's understanding of his faith.

This tablet in the dome of St. Peter's commemorates the Pontificate of Pius IX.

Looking up at the dome of St. Peter's. The tablet was erected in the Pontificate of Pius XII.

The tomb of the beloved Pontiff Pius XII.

The Gathering of the Cardinals

When Pope Pius XII died at Castel Gandolfo on October 9, 1958, he was assured of a high place in the history of the Papacy. In a Pontificate of nearly twenty years duration, he had proved himself a worthy custodian of the keys of St. Peter, a man of great wisdom and courage. Coming to his high office on the very eve of the most disastrous war in the history of man, he had guided the Church through a period in which humanity itself seemed to be at the test. Catholics and non-Catholics alike had learned to respect his judgment and his utterances, and the world genuinely mourned his death.

For three days his body lay in state, while the world spoke and read of his achievements and remembered the last years of his life, when he grew in saintliness. The funeral of the great Pope was solemn and awe-inspiring. Led by a crucifer bearing a golden cross, a procession of Church dignitaries bore the body of Eugenio Pacelli to its last resting place.

The clergy of Rome led the procession in honor of their dead bishop, all of them in their white surplices. They were followed by the canons of St. Peter's in crimson capes, and the Julian Choir, a hundred voices strong, singing the heart-stirring *Miserere*:

"Have mercy on me. O Lord, according to thine own mercy."

The pallbearers were escorted by the Swiss Guards in their bright uniforms of blue and orange, and they were followed by the Chamberlains of the Cape and Sword, with high ruffs around their throats, and the officers of the Noble Guard with their brilliant uniforms. Behind the cortege walked twenty-two cardinals in their mourning robes of purple.

The body of the dead Pope was placed beside his triple coffin and the chant of the service began. The vicar of St. Peter's blessed the body, and asked God not to "deliver him into the hands of the enemy, nor forget him forever, but command him to be taken up by the Holy Angels, to be borne to our home in Paradise."

Then the body was lifted into the triple coffin. Each cardinal came forward in turn and sprinkled it with holy water from an aspergillum and gave his final blessing to the beloved Pontiff.

The eulogy, in Latin, was delivered by Monsignor Bacci, whose duty it would soon be to call upon the cardinals in the ancient tongue to elect his successor. Then the triple coffin was closed, and officially sealed by the Cardinal Camerlengo, the arch-priest of St. Peter's, and two other prelates. It was then removed to the front of the altar and swung down into the crypt below, where it was placed in a simple white marble sarcophagus, to rest near the grave of St. Peter himself.

And now the great Pope was "truly dead," and in the tradition of the Church the cardinal-electors must be called to secret session to choose a new Pope. The conclave has justly come by its name, for the cardinals are truly locked up *cum clave* in the Latin phrase, or "with a key," while they deliberate.

The tradition of the conclave goes back to the thirteenth century. When Pope Clement IV died in his palace in Viterbo, north of Rome, in 1268, eighteen Cardinals met in the palace to elect his successor. But they could not reach agreement, and weeks became months and months became years, while the Medieval world waited for his successor. The people of Viterbo adopted the ancient Roman practice of locking up the electors, to hold them prisoner until they had reached a decision. The entrances to the palace were sealed by stone masons, leaving only a single tiny door, through which the cardinals were given their daily ration of bread and water. This produced the desired result, and after a lapse of nearly three and a half years, the Church had a new Pope, Theobald Visconti, who reigned as Gregory X.

Pope Gregory X was thus well aware of the dangers of a long interregnum, and in 1274, he issued his Apostolic Convention, which designated the sealed "conclave" as the means by which the election of the Popes would thenceforward be conducted. While there have been minor alterations in the rules from time to time, in basic outline the traditional ceremonies of the conclave have remained unchanged for seven centuries.

With the death of Pope Pius XII, the fifty-four cardinals of the Church were under orders to proceed immediately to Rome, under the provisions of the Apostolic Constitution which Pope Pius had issued himself on December 8, 1945. Pope Pius XI had increased the interval between the death of a Pope and the start of a conclave from ten to fifteen days, or even eighteen if necessary, in order to allow sufficient time for all the cardinals to gather in Rome.

With Cardinal Mindszenty and Cardinal Stepinac confined within the borders of Hungary and Yugoslavia, only fifty-two cardinals could participate in the election, and the death of Cardinal Mooney reduced to fifty-one the number of electors who were seated in the Sistine Chapel as the conclave opened. Seventeen of the number were Italian, six French, three Brazilian, three Spanish, two Portuguese, two from the Oriental rite, two Argentinian, two German, two Canadian, two Amer-

Elia Cardinal dalla Costa, Archbishop of Florence, Italy.

Maurizio Cardinal Fossati, Archbishop of Turin, Italy.

ican, and one each from Australia, Belgium, Chile, China, Cuba, Ecuador, Ireland, Poland, Colombia, and India.

As the conclave was called to order, it represented the culmination of preparations in the most minute detail that had started immediately upon the death of Pope Pius XII. When the Papal throne is vacated, the Papal power remains suspended. The cardinals become the trustees of Papal authority, without the power to exercise it. Only upon the election of a new Pope does the Papal power again find full exercise. During the vacancy, or "interregnum," only the routine work of the Vatican proceeds; no new policy may be determined and no new agreements with foreign states may be entered into. The head of the Apostolic Chamber administers the necessary material affairs of the Vatican during this period, and the Cardinal Camerlengo is assisted by three different cardinals each day in the performance of his necessary duties.

The Cardinal Camerlengo is also the head of the College of Cardinals during the interregnum. It is his duty to confirm the death of the Pope, which he does in a traditional ceremony: drawing back the white cloth covering the face of the dead Pope, addressing him three times by his Christian name. Receiving no answer upon the third call, he then announces to the assemblage, in Latin: "The Pope is truly dead." With these words the vacancy in the Papacy is officially announced.

When the cardinals were assembled in Rome, they were convened in General Congregation. At this meeting, the *Vacantis Apostolicae Sedis,* issued by Pope Pius XII in 1945, was read. The conclave would be governed by the rules set forth in this document, and all of the cardinals took an oath to observe these edicts faithfully. Each cardinal took an oath that he would not be influenced by any temporal power attempting to sway his vote, that he would maintain unbroken secrecy regarding the proceedings of the conclave and the balloting, that he would not use the telephone, transmitting devices, cameras or recorders during the conclave, and that if he himself were elected Pope, he would not give up the temporal rights of the Apostolic See, by which the independence of the Vatican is maintained.

Under the direction of the General Congregation, the physical preparations for the conclave went forward. Following the ancient tradition, a part of the Vatican Palace was sealed off by bricking up the entrances. Within the sealed-off area, small rooms, or "cells," were provided for each of the cardinal-electors. Each cardinal was permitted two attendants, lay or clerical. Most of the cardinals brought a secretary and a servant. The rooms were assigned by drawing lots.

While the cardinals were not restricted to a bread-and-water diet, as were their thirteenth-century predecessors, a simple regimen was provided. The cells were small rooms, each fitted out very simply with only a bed and the most necessary articles of furniture. All the outside windows in the conclave area were painted over with an opaque blue paint, and the kitchens were stocked with foods that would supply a simple diet for the duration of the conclave.

In the Sistine Chapel, where the balloting would take place, all necessary prep-

Teodosio Clemente Cardinal de Gouveia, Archbishop of Lourenço Marques, Portuguese East Africa.

The coat-of-arms of Pope John XXIII.

The coat-of-arms of Pope Pius XII.

arations were now completed. At the altar six candles were placed and upon the altar was placed a large chalice covered with a thin gold plate to receive the ballots. The Papal throne had been removed and chairs had been set in place for the cardinal-electors. Each chair had been surmounted by a purple canopy, to indicate that each elector had equal status with all others until the moment when a Pope had been elected. At that time all of the canopies, except that of the new Pope, would be lowered, thus signifying the obedience of the cardinals to the Pope-elect.

Since the proceedings of the conclave are secret, only the most necessary personnel are admitted, and these are sworn to secrecy. They included the Sacristan of the Apostolic Palace, six Masters of Ceremonies, the secretary of the College of Cardinals, a member of a religious order to serve as confessor, physicians, pharmacists and such other personnel as might be necessary to serve the needs of the electors.

The conclave began in deepest solemnity. To the ordinarily solemn air of such proceedings had been added the sadness occasioned by the death of Cardinal Mooney, unexpectedly, just a brief time before the sessions were scheduled to begin. On the morning of that day, the Cardinal Dean Eugene Tisserant celebrated a votive Mass of the Holy Spirit at the Altar of the Chair in St. Peter's. The cardinal-electors arrived in a solemn procession escorted by members of the Noble Guard and the Swiss Guard.

When the impressive ceremony had been completed, Monsignor Bacci, acting as Secretary of Briefs to Princes, delivered the traditional sermon, the "exhortation," in Latin to the assembled electors. Addressing the Cardinals as "most eminent fathers," he outlined the needs of the Papacy and the qualities which must be sought in a Pontiff in our times:

"Twenty years ago in this chapel, in the presence of the Sacred College of Cardinals, I preached a sermon on the election of a new Pope. At that time I little dreamed that after a span of years filled with grave events, I would at your bidding speak again on the same subject.

"In the gathering of the Senate of the Church which immediately convened, the man whose name was in the minds and on the lips of everyone was chosen as Head of the Church of Jesus Christ. The entire Christian world joyfully and confidently turned to him, as with a sure and firm hand he assumed the guidance of the ship of Peter. He was not afraid of the waves of the swelling sea; he did not fear the blustery storms; he did not tremble at the deluge of lies and errors. The truly gigantic difficulties of the times and the obstacles placed in his path by men were unable to hinder or delay his long, sleepless, studious devotion. While all about him the whole social order seemed uncertain, tottering and ready to collapse, he alone, because he trusted in God and relied on His help, proceeded safely on his way. He devoted his energies not merely to the eternal salvation of all men, but to the task of procuring harmony, peace and prosperity for all classes of men and for human society itself. Because of this the opinion was widespread that no other man could govern the Church of God with equal wisdom, prudence and courage in such demanding times.

"Nevertheless, by the hidden designs of God, which we may not attempt to explore and are utterly unable to fathom, it came to pass that he who had won the deep love and admiration of all men and seemed worthy of being allowed to live forever, was summoned to enter into the reward which he so richly deserved.

"Your present task then, Most Eminent Fathers, is to provide for the welfare of the bereaved Church by selecting as Supreme Pontiff a man who will be altogether worthy of such a predecessor. This is indeed a great and formidable task. You are beyond doubt equal to this task by reason of your eminent intelligence, learning and prudence in practical affairs. What then can I, who am so far inferior to you in station, rank and talent, point out to you that you do not already profoundly know? How can I exhort you, I who have no authority in this matter except what you yourselves have kindly delegated to me?

"I shall therefore be content merely to propose for your consideration what should be the qualities of the future Pontiff, so that as soon as possible you may choose the man whom our times demand.

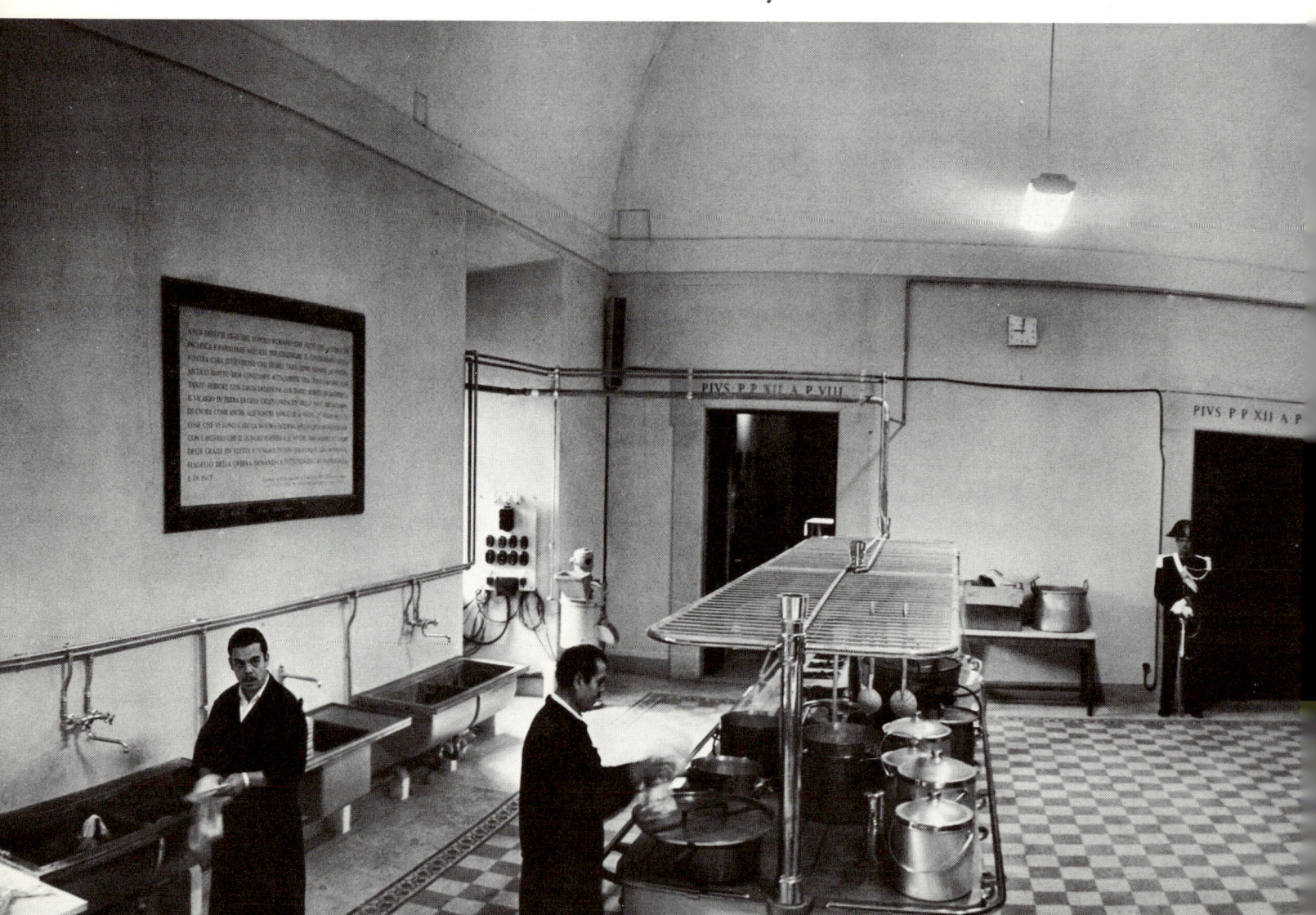

The kitchen is made ready for the conclave.

Enrique Cardinal Pla y Deniel, Archbishop of Toledo and Primate of Spain.

"You are well acquainted with the times in which we live. They are indeed no better than those in which Pius XII, our late lamented Pontiff, carried on his sacred office. The long, bitter war, which burst into a fearful blaze at the beginning of his Pontificate, has now come to an end. However, the causes which launched this war have apparently not been laid to rest. In many regions there exist great tensions, fighting and rioting; and where actual violence seems to have subsided, things are nevertheless not altogether peaceful. Why so many nations are torn apart with bitter quarrels is not hard to understand. Individual men and whole nations can start wars but they can not bring about a peace that will be sincere and based on a solid foundation except by the inspiration of God. By the law and teaching of the Gospel man is not, as Plautus says, 'a wolf to his fellow man,' but men ought to be brothers. If therefore we can all love one another with a mutual charity, there can never arise a new Cain to shed his brother's blood. It can never happen that one people will rise to make war upon another. It is perfectly plain to everyone

The three American conclavists: Cardinals Spellman, Mooney, and McIntyre.

that from strife and war nothing can result but smoking ruins and a mountain of miseries common to all, to victors and vanquished alike. For as divine charity nourished by religion unites and pacifies men, so hatred, which easily breaks out because of unbridled ambition and an excessive love of aggrandizing oneself and one's own nation, blinds the minds of men and can even drive them to the point of adopting insane counsels from which can come only fresh disasters for the human race.

"Therefore, the man whom you will select as Pontiff, like him whose death we mourn, must necessarily excel in all such gifts and virtues as will enamble him to conciliate and unite men, races and nations among themselves, and at the same time provide him with skill and influence to revive and foster the Christian religion as widely as possible, in both private and public spheres of action. For if God is relegated to second place and if those principles which come from the Gospels are rejected, every human effort, no matter how praiseworthy, is certainly doomed to failure.

"There is another consideration which you must carefully weigh. Today in many countries famous for their long history, populous, and renowned for their Christian and secular culture, religion, the only sound foundation for human society, is harassed by clever artifices, by open or hidden indictments and even by the most bitter persecution. Almost no possibility is left for the Church to live by her own laws. Her sacred rights are trampled underfoot. Many of her pastors have been thrown into prison or have been so interfered with that they are prevented from feeding their flocks. Even in your sacred College, and this is your highest honor and glory, there are some who share misfortunes of this sort and with God's help bear them with unconquered fortitude. But what most afflicts good men with bitter sorrow is this: They see whole nations deprived of legitimate bishops to rule and teach them with due freedom. They see them without schools and colleges in which young people may be formed to Christian truth and virtue. They see them lacking newspapers and periodicals in which truth and the rights of the Church may be defended. They see them languishing in this miserable state although with the divine grace they hold tenaciously to the faith of their fathers. It is clear that those who have gained supreme power in these nations are trying by every malicious means to reduce the Church to slavery, so that thereafter if possible they may the more easily undermine and completely destroy it.

"This extremely grave situation demands, Most Eminent Fathers, that the new Pontiff whom we await excel in courage of spirit and the most ardent charity. To all men, whether they wish to listen or they do not, let him openly propose the truth. Let him with invincible heart protect the sacred rights of the Church. Let him tremble before no enemy of the most high God or of our holy religion. Let him as far as he can console his sons and brothers who are oppressed by unjust tyranny, and let him rouse in them the hope of winning their due liberty. Let him with paternal heart and with every means at his command call back to the one fold of Jesus Christ those peoples who are unfortunately separated from Him and who lie in the darkness of error. Let him, finally, love with intense charity those who are enemies of the very name of Christian, and let him look upon them as prodigal and wandering sons and yearn with all his heart for the day that will bring them back to the home of the one common Father.

"Moreover—and this you know well—as in the past so also today untruths of all sorts, clothed as it were in new garments and often disguised under the appearance of truth, spawn one from another and lead the minds of man into error. Let the new Pontiff uncover these errors and with the apostolic authority that can not be mistaken let him score and condemn them. Let him in season and out of season warn all Christians away from poisoned pastures. Let him illumine their minds with the light of truth and let him rule, strengthen and confirm their morals.

"Let him be a highly skilled teacher in the Universal Church. Today especially, because of the flood of newspapers and pamphlets, because of moving pictures which are sometimes evil or dangerous and are viewed by countless multitudes, because of the wonderful invention of television by which distant scenes, events, the human voice invade the very privacy of the home, because of all these powerful media, minds and wills particularly of youth can be disturbed and more effectively than ever before allured to error and vice. Therefore it is clear how necessary it is not only to defend the Christian community from so many dangers but also to bring it about that the new arts of communication which our age has invented be adapted to the service of virtue and the salvation of souls.

"It seems then that these words of Jeremiah the prophet may well be applied to the new Pontiff: 'Behold, I have entrusted my message to thy lips; lo, I have set thee today over the nations and over kingdoms to root up and to pull down, to build and to plant.' He must root up errors and vices and destroy them. He must likewise build up and adorn the structure of truth. Let him sow as widely as possible the seeds of Christian virtue that they may sprout into sanctity and propagate and promote everywhere on earth the kingdom of God.

"Besides, he must be a most energetic shepherd. He must possess great knowledge. He must know thoroughly the laws that govern international affairs. He must be outstanding for prudence in action. But that is not all. He must bear in himself the Divine Image of Him who said, 'I am the good shepherd. The good shepherd gives his life for his sheep. I am the good shepherd and I know mine and mine know me.' Let him be a bishop of souls. Wherefore, if he know by actual experience the present needs of the nations, the dangers which must be warded off, the disputes that must be settled, if he has not merely been immersed in books but has lived at the very heart of human affairs, if he burns with such an intense charity that he desires to give his life for the sheep entrusted to him, then beyond a doubt he can claim to be that most perfect image of a Supreme Pontiff which is the object of your hearts' desire.

"Let him most graciously receive into his presence the bishops whom the Holy Spirit has placed to rule the Church of God. Let him assist them in their doubts and needs, yet him console them in their trals, let him promote their undertakings with all his strength.

"Let him embrace with equal fatherly affection the Western and the Eastern Churches. Let him hear with all the sympathy at his command the petitions and the desires which come to the See of St. Peter from the whole world.

"Let the Pontiff whom you will select exercise the office of a teacher who is not only a shepherd but also a most loving father. For as you well know, when a man is raised to the lofty eminence of the Supreme Pontificate, he belongs not to himself nor to a particular people or nation but to all the people which the Catholic Church embraces. Therefore he must have a great heart, that kind of heart which our Divine Redeemer Jesus possessed. He may well repeat this thought of the Apostle of the Gentiles: 'Who is weak and I am not weak? Who is scandalized and I am not on fire?' For the charity of Christ presses us. Therefore let him turn his head and his heart to those people especially who are oppressed by persecution and tyrannical power, to those whose lot is cast in the lowliest rank of society, finally to that multitude of persons who possess nothing or very little of the goods of this world, so that not even by their labor and the sweat of their brow can they win for themselves food and shelter. To these let him turn his mind and his heart. Let him hold nothing more dear or more agreeable than to wipe away their tears, relieve their anxieties and raise them to a better and more just condition. Following the example of Jesus Christ, let him espouse the cause of the poor, those who live by their daily labor and those especially who do not have enough to support a growing family. May he be able at long last to bring into actual practice, not merely by teaching but also by persuasion, advice and untiring effort, those rights of human labor which the Roman Pontiffs in their encyclical letters

Gregory Peter XV Cardinal Agagianian, Patriarch of the Armenians.

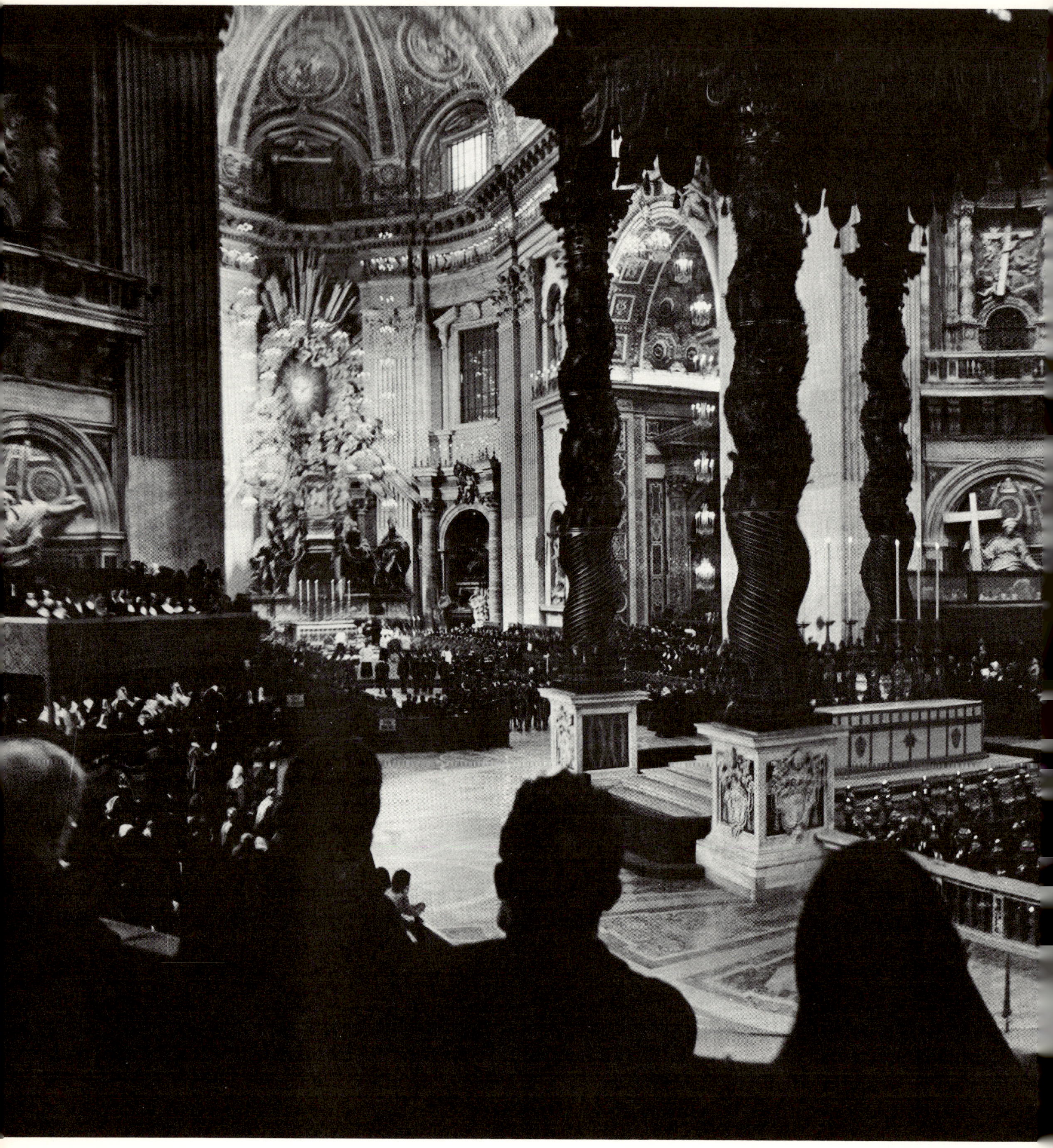

The Mass of the Holy Spirit in St. Peter's Basilica was attended by the cardinals
prior to the opening of the conclave.

Ignatius Gabriel Cardinal Tappouni, Syrian Patriarch of Antioch.

have long since approved. It is a dangerous thing, as you well know, to neglect and ignore the rights of man and to trample underfoot the principles of social justice which are rooted in both the letter and the spirit of the Gospel of Christ.

"The word pontifex, pontiff, as you know, comes from the Latin word *pons*, a bridge. Let our new Pontiff therefore be a bridge between evil men and good men, so that he may bring the one class to better life and the other to a higher virtue. Let him be a bridge between the various classes of men and bring it about that there flourish a more ample justice among them and that a more ardent charity prevail. Let him be a bridge joining all nations, even those who either reject the Catholic religion or dare to persecute it, and let him successfully lead them to establish a sincere peace, the source of true prosperity.

"With all these gifts of mind and heart, Most Eminent Fathers, may he be adorned whom you will by your votes raise to the height of the Supreme Pontificate. But may he be resplendent above all with priestly virtues and holiness of life. Natural endowments have real value, but they can not supply all that is requisite for meeting the challenge of so great an office. Surely, if the future Pontiff possesses outstanding holiness, he will be able to obtain from God all that is necessary to govern the Universal Church.

"The great French orator, Jacques Bénigne Bossuet, while delivering the funeral oration over a dead king, said, 'No one can really be called great, except God alone.' However, even in this mortal life, the man who, because of his exalted office, bears in himself the image of God as the Vicar of Jesus Christ can and should really be called great. Such undoubtedly will be the one whom you will soon elect, and although he ought to be adorned with countless and matchless gifts, you nevertheless, with the enlightenment of the Divine Spirit, will discover a man who is worthy of this great honor and strong enough to bear his heavy burden.

"For my part, Most Eminent Fathers, there is nothing more to say except to beg your kind indulgence for the inadequate way in which I have delivered my message to you, and at the same time to assure you that in union with all children of the Catholic Church, I shall petition the Divine Redeemer and His most holy Mother that your minds may be illumined by the heavenly light and that your wills be moved by the inspiration of divine grace to elect him as the Supreme Head of the Church whom our troubled times demand and whom all good men earnestly await."

Thus charged with their great mission in this profound and movingly eloquent appeal, the electors prepared for the task before them. On the afternoon of Saturday, October 25, they gathered in solemn procession to enter the conclave. One elector, the Chinese Cardinal Tien-Ken-Sin, was so feeble that he was brought to the Vatican Palace by ambulance and reached his cell by elevator. In the balloting his vote was taken in his room by "infirmarians" assigned to this task.

The cardinals, each dressed in violet cassock and mozzetta, proceeded to the Pauline Chapel, escorted by two members of the Swiss Guard. The Noble Guard was also in attendance, in full military array, adding to the splendor of the scene. The Papal choir sang the *Veni Creator Spiritus* and the procession of cardinals moved toward the Sistine Chapel.

When the cardinals had entered the Chapel, Cardinal Dean Tisserant said the Collect *Deus qui corda fidelium* at the altar. Then came the ancient and traditional announcement of *extra omnes,* bidding all those without authority to leave the conclave. The Cardinal Camerlengo and the three Cardinals of the Particular

CONCLAVE 1958

E.MO CARD. SPELLMAN

CELLA N. 46

INGRESSO Scala della Galleria Lapidaria

PIANO ultimo.

Room assignment: Cardinal Spellman's card assigned him to room 46, on the top floor.

Congregation made a tour of the conclave area to attest that all precautions had been taken and all openings sealed as required and as a final gesture they closed and locked the last open door. At 6:08 P.M. the bell in the Court of St. Damasus tolled three times to signal that the conclave had been sealed against all outside intrusion.

The first day of the conclave began with the community Mass in the Pauline Chapel. This Mass is traditionally celebrated by the Dean or the Senior Cardinal and all the members of the Sacred College receive Holy Communion. After the completion of this service the electors returned to their cells to take their morning meal. The morning routine on succeeding days varied somewhat from the first day's procedure. Each cardinal said Mass in his own cell at whatever time suited him best, and a community Mass was offered each morning by the Bishop-Sacristan for cardinals who wished to attend.

The routine for the rest of each day did not vary. After Mass and the morning meal the electors proceeded to the election hall for the morning balloting. At the close of the morning session, the cardinals returned to their cells, where the noonday meal was served separately to each of them. Following the custom of the Latin countries, the cardinals were then permitted a period for a brief "siesta," and after this the electors had time for a stroll in the corridors. At mid-afternoon, usually between three and four o'clock, all reassembled for the afternoon "scrutiny" or balloting. This was followed by a period during which any necessary business of the conclave, aside from the election, could be transacted, and if required a formal meeting of the College of Cardinals could be called. The evening meal was served between nine and ten o'clock, and upon its completion a bell was tolled and the traditional call was heard, *In cellam, Domini*—"Into your cells, my lords." If a cardinal did not wish to be disturbed in his room, he ordered two bars of wood placed before his door in the form of a St. Andrew's cross.

The balloting took place in strictest conformity with the rules of secrecy of the conclave. Since each participant is sworn to eternal secrecy and since no outsiders are permitted within the conclave, no record of the individual balloting may be reported and in fact no record is ever made. As the count of each balloting is concluded and verified, the ballots are burned, and the individual counts are lost to history.

Three forms of election are provided for. The first is "per inspirationem"—by inspiration, when the cardinals by unanimous acclamation designate their choice without formal ballot. This of course is a very rare occurrence, the last incidence of this event having been in 1154 when Pope Hadrian IV was elected. The second form of election, also rare, is "per compromisum"—by compromise. In this form the cardinals select a committee of three, five, or seven electors who in turn select the Pope, the entire assembly agreeing to bound by the choice of the committee.

A guard poses in full regalia as the work of sealing off the conclave area proceeds.

The third, and usual, form of election is "per scrutinium"—by ballot, and it is by this method that Pope John XXIII was elected. The ballots are of paper, oblong in shape, printed in advance with the prescribed form:

> Eligo in Summum Pontificem R. Meum D. Card.
> _____

or in translation: "I elect as Supreme Pontiff the Most Reverend, My Lord Cardinal _____"

As each cardinal inscribes the name of his choice on the ballot, he folds the sheet once. Then, in the prescribed order, the cardinals arise and carry their ballots up to the altar, where a chalice has been placed to receive the folded ballots. Each cardinal, as he approaches the altar, kneels a moment in prayer, then rises and pronounces in Latin this solemn oath: "I call to witness Jesus Christ, who will judge me, that I am electing him who before God I judge should be elected."

Having taken this oath before his colleagues, he then places the ballot on the paten and slides it into the chalice. When all the cardinals have voted, the ballots are removed and counted, to be sure that their number corresponds to the number of cardinals eligible to vote. (In the event the tally is not correct the ballots are immediately burned and the voting recommences.)

If the number of ballots removed from the chalice is correct, a tally of the ballots is then taken, and the number of votes cast for each nominee is announced. If any candidate has received two-thirds of the ballots cast plus one, he is declared elected. If no candidate has received the required number of votes, preparations are made to resume the balloting, and the procedure is again followed from the beginning.

In order to assure the accuracy and truth of the count, three tellers tally and announce the results of each ballot, and the ballots are tallied twice and rechecked. Upon the completion of each tally and the proper certification of the result, the ballots are strung together with a needle and are put aside to be burned.

The results of the balloting are announced to those who wait outside in St. Peter's Square in the ancient and traditional manner. As the cardinals continue their balloting in the Sistine Chapel, the tallied ballots are burned in an old-fashioned stove set up for that purpose. When the balloting has been inconclusive and there is not yet a new Pope, the ballots are burned with wet straw, giving forth a

ORDO CONCLAVIS

SABBATO, DIE 25 OCTOBRIS 1958

Mane

1. Eṁi Domini Cardinales ad Sacrarium Basilicae Vaticanae hora 9.15 accedent.

2. Eṁus Card. Eugenius Tisserant, Episcopus Ostiensis, Portuensis et S. Rufinae ac Decanus Sacri Collegii, Missam solemnem *de Spiritu Sancto* celebrabit in Basilica Vaticana hora 9.30.

Eṁi Cardinales, vestibus laneis, rocheto simplici et cappis laneis violaceis sine pellibus ermellineis induti, adsistent.

Post Missam habebitur oratio *de eligendo Summo Pontifice*.

Vespere

3. Eṁi Cardinales, cum suis Conclavistis, hora 15.30 ad Palatium Vaticanum advenient.

Hora 16 Eṁi Patres, vestibus et mozzetta violaceis laneis cum zona serica eiusdem coloris et rocheto simplici conveniunt in Sacellum Paulinum, et facta oratione, processionaliter Conclave ingrediuntur. Magister Caeremoniarum, Crucem Papalem ferens, procedit: sequuntur Cardinales iuxta ordinem praecedentiae; Crucem praecedunt familiares Cardinalium, et immediate cantores hymnum *Veni Creator* cantantes; post Cardinales sequuntur Praelati. Cum in Sacellum Sixtinum pervenerint, Cardinalis Decanus apud altare dicit orationem *Deus qui corda fidelium*, qua absoluta Praefectus Caeremoniarum intimat *extra omnes* e Sacello.

4. Legitur Constitutio « Vacantis Sedis Apostolicae » Pii Pp. XII (praetermissis iis quae res iam peractas respiciunt).

Conclave schedule: The details of each day's program were carefully prepared in advance.

This is the first page of the official schedule.

A workman bricking up a window to seal off the conclave area
following the centuries old custom.

dense black smoke, easily visible to the watchers in the Square through the tall narrow chimney. However, when the balloting has been successful, and a new Pope has been elected, the ballots are burned with crisp dry straw, giving forth a fine white smoke.

Since the ballots are immediately burned, and the oath of secrecy prevents any record of the voting from reaching the public, we can only surmise the events of

Final preparations are made to assure the secrecy and isolation of the conclave.

PREFETTURA
DELLE
CEREMONIE APOSTOLICHE

DISPOSIZIONI
per il vestiario da usarsi dagli Em.mi Signori Cardinali
e dalla loro Corte durante il Conclave

Gli Eminentissimi Signori Cardinali nella Messa privata *De Spiritu Sancto*, che ascolteranno nei giorni del Conclave, e durante gli Scrutinî, useranno la sottana violacea, il rocchetto liscio e la mozzetta violacea di lana, con fascia con fiocchi d'oro e la Croce pettorale con il consueto cordone rosso-oro.

Faranno portare anche la Cappa di seta violacea senza pelli di ermellino, il rocchetto griccio, e la fascia violacea di seta ondata con i fiocchi d'oro che indosseranno nella seconda adorazione dell'Eletto Pontefice.

I Conclavisti useranno sempre la sottana ed il ferraiolone di color nero, e porteranno seco una cotta per l'assistenza alla Messa privata del proprio Emo Cardinale.

I domestici indosseranno vestito nero con calzone lungo e cravatta bianca, e porteranno anche il frack.

Gli Eminentissimi Signori Cardinali si rendono avvisati che nella prima mattina del Conclave, alle ore 8.30, la Messa letta *De Spiritu Sancto*, alla quale tutti gli Emi dovranno assistere, sarà celebrata dall'Emo Signor Cardinale Decano.

20 ottobre 1958.

per mandato del Sacro Collegio

ENRICO DANTE
Prot. Ap., Prefetto delle Cerimonie Pontificie

Correct dress: Instructions from the Prefect of Pontifical Ceremonies of the Sacred College established the correct attire at all times during the conclave.

This sealed window is a symbol of the secrecy and the purity of the conclave.

The last entrance to the conclave area is sealed off by a symbolic chain.

DISPOSIZIONI PER I CONCLAVISTI

1. I Conclavisti entreranno nel Palazzo Apostolico del Conclave il 25 ottobre alle ore 15,30.

2. Alle ore 16,30 si riuniranno nella Cappella Paolina, ove il Segretario del Conclave, e il Prefetto delle Cerimonie, dopo averne fatto l'appello, ammetteranno al giuramento per delega dell'Emo Card. Camerlengo, prima i sacerdoti, poi i laici per categorie e per lingua.

3. I Conclavisti sacerdoti celebreranno la Messa nelle varie Cappelle dopo la celebrazione degli Emi Cardinali.

4. Il pranzo avrà luogo alle 13; per i Conclavisti nelle varie sale del Quartiere della Guardia Palatina.

5. Alle ore 16,15 di ciascun giorno, a cominciare dal 26 ottobre, i Conclavisti si recheranno nella Cappella *Matilde* per la recita del Rosario e la Benedizione Eucaristica.

6. Durante gli scrutini rimarranno nelle proprie stanze, o nelle Logge.

7. Tutti, come si è certi, terranno contegno edificante e si mostreranno ossequenti alle disposizioni, che verranno date per mezzo del Segretario del S. Collegio, ed eviteranno qualunque raggruppamento non necessario.

Dal Palazzo Apostolico Vaticano, 23 ottobre 1958.

Mons. A. Di Jorio
Segretario del S. Collegio.

Instructions to conclavists to appear for the administration of the oath of secrecy.

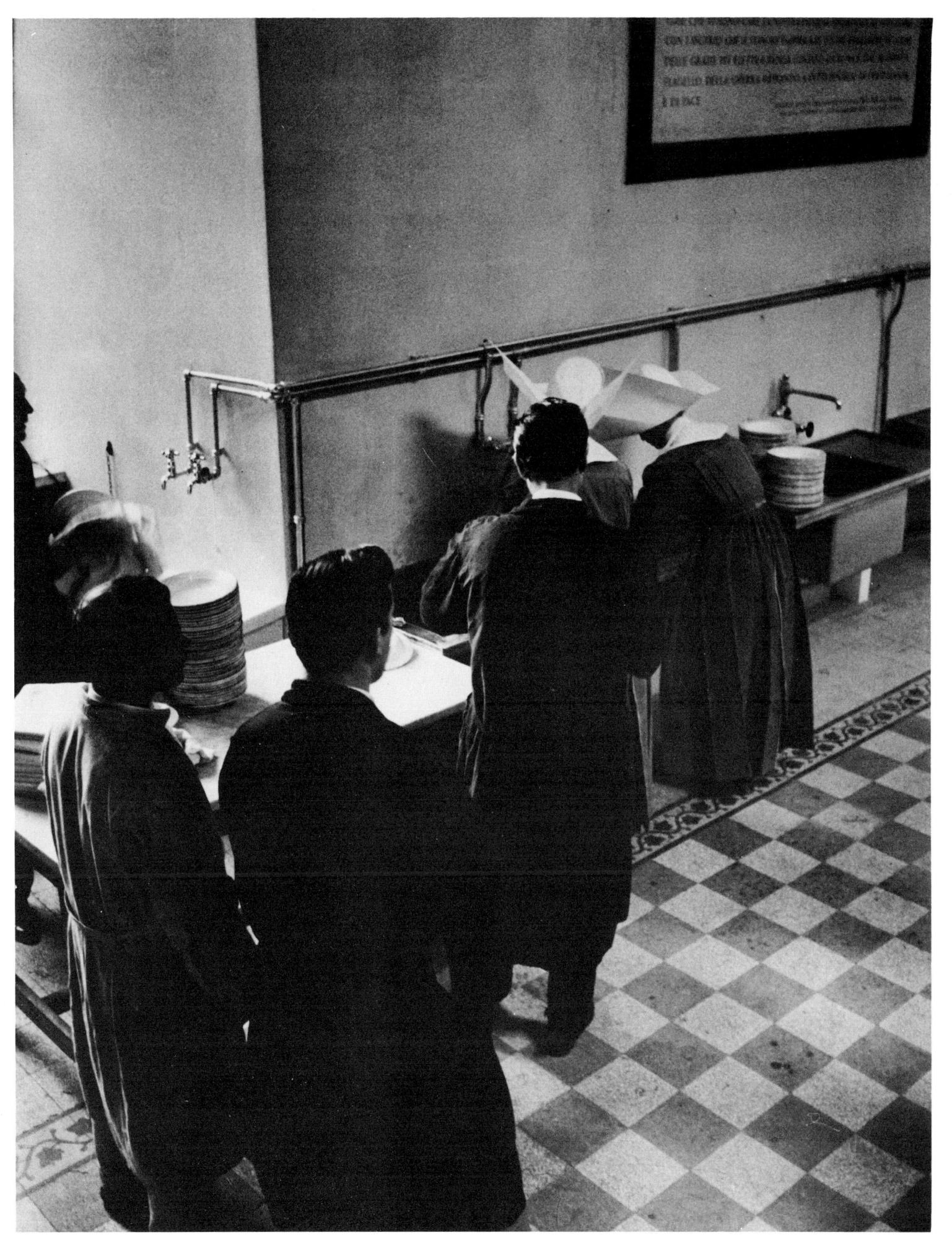

In this kitchen the simple meals were prepared for the conclavists.

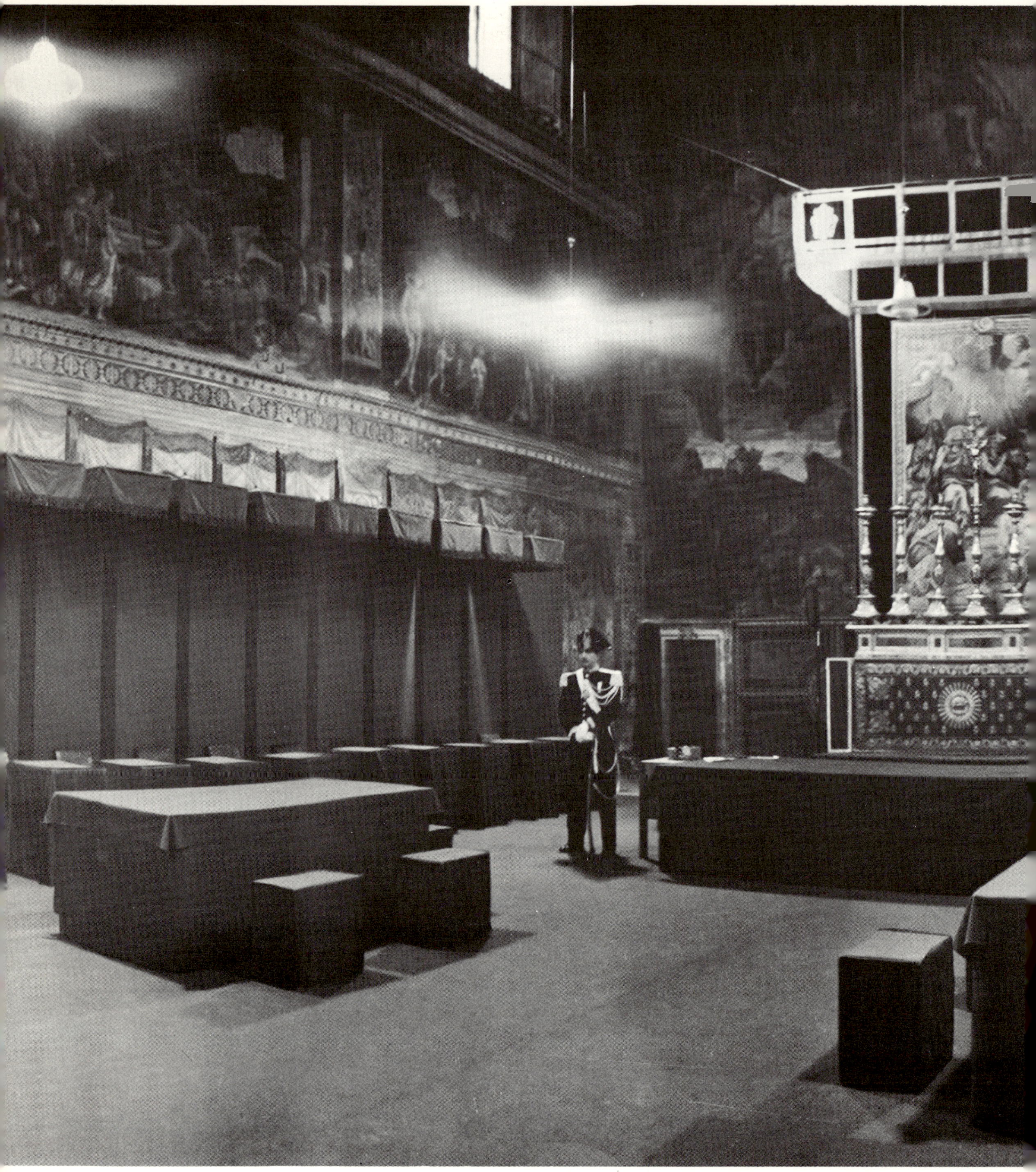

The Sistine Chapel, prepared for the conclave and the balloting to elect a new Pope.

FORMULA IURISIURANDI

a Magistris Caeremoniarum atque ab omnibus aliis Conclavistis ecclesiasticis praestandi, una vel altera die ante ingressum in Conclave.

Ego ....

constitutus coram te ....

tactis per me Sanctis Dei Evangeliis coram me positis, promitto et iuro me inviolabile servaturum esse secretum in omnibus et singulis, quae de novi Pontificis electione in Cardinalium Congregationibus acta vel decreta sint et in Conclavi seu in loco electionis aguntur, scrutinium directe vel indirecte respicientia, quaeque omnia quovis modo cognoverim, adeo ut nec directe, nec indirecte, neque nutu, neque verbo, neque scriptis, vel alias quomodolibet, ipsum mihi violare liceat; itemque promitto et iuro me ullo modo in Conclavi usurum esse instrumentis quibuslibet ad vocem transmittendam vel recipiendam, vel ad imagines luce exprimendas quovis modo aptis, et hoc nedum sub poena excommunicationis latae sententiae, futuro Pontifici speciali modo reservatae, privative etiam quoad Sacram Poenitentiariam, sed etiam sub poena privationis cuiuscumque beneficii, pensionis, officii vel muneris ipso facto incurrendae in casu transgressionis. Quod secretum accuratissime ac religiose servabo etiam post peractam novi Pontificis electionem, nisi ab eodem Pontifice peculiaris facultas aut expressa dispensatio mihi concessa fuerit.

Pariter promitto et iuro nullo modo a quavis civili potestate, quovis praetextu, munus proponendi Veto seu Exclusivam, etiam sub forma simplicis desiderii, esse recepturum, ipsumque hoc Veto, qualibet ratione mihi cognitum, patefacturum, sive universo Cardinalium Collegio simul congregato, sive singulis Cardinalibus, sive scripto, sive ore, sive directe ac proxime, sive oblique ac per alios, sive ante ingressum in Conclave, sive ipso perdurante; nullique interventui, intercessioni, aliive cuilibet modo, quo laicae potestates cuiuslibet gradus et ordinis voluerint sese in Pontificis electione immiscere, auxilium vel favorem praestiturum.

Sic me Deus adiuvet et haec sancta Dei Evangelia, quae propriis manibus tango.

The form of the oath of secrecy administered to all the conclavists and ecclesiastical attendants. A somewhat different form was used for lay attendants.

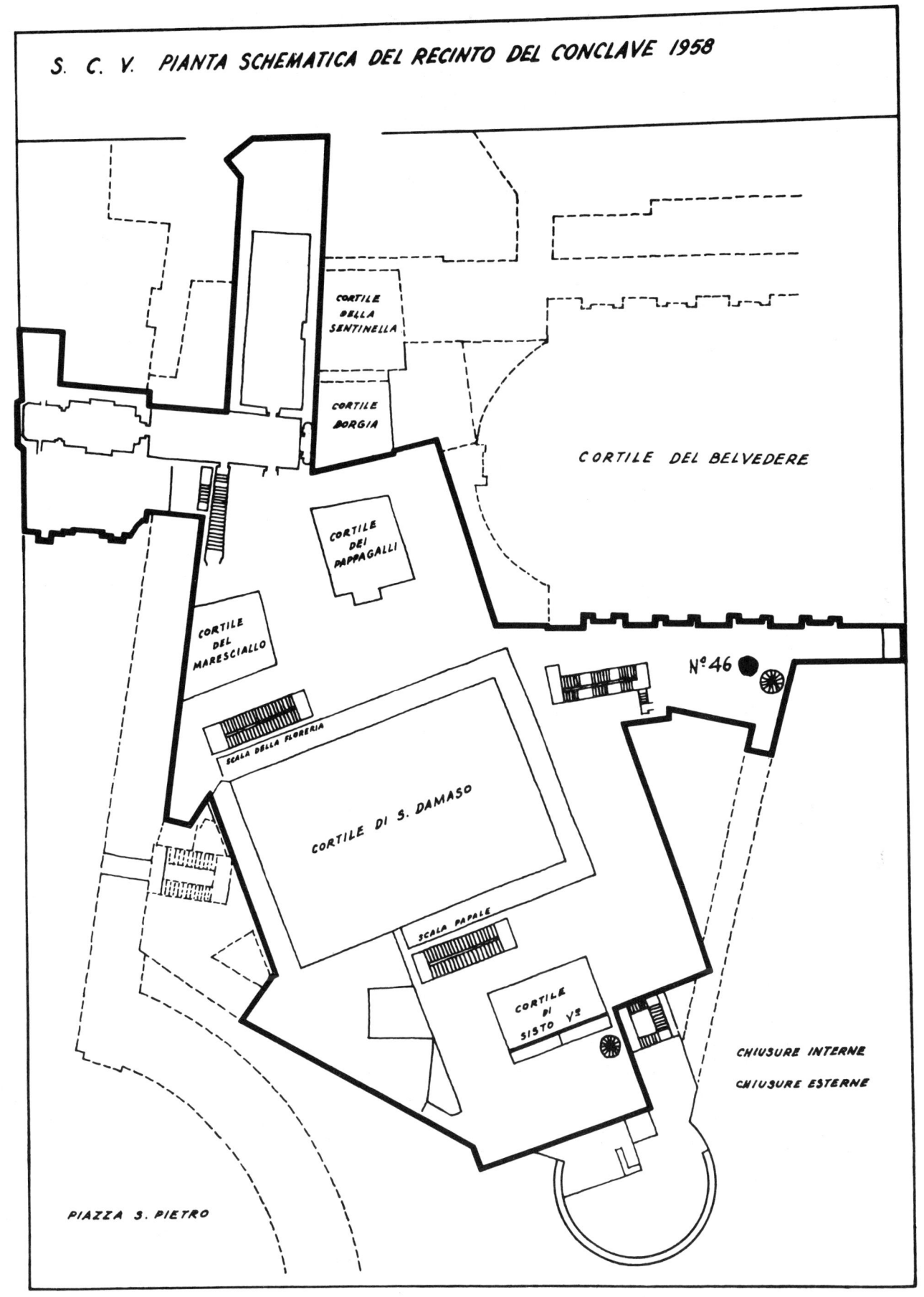

Schematic drawing of the 1958 Conclave Area.

This was the means by which news of the conclave was given to the world outside.

This vertical panoramic photograph shows the famous stove and the chimney leading out of the Sistine Chapel.

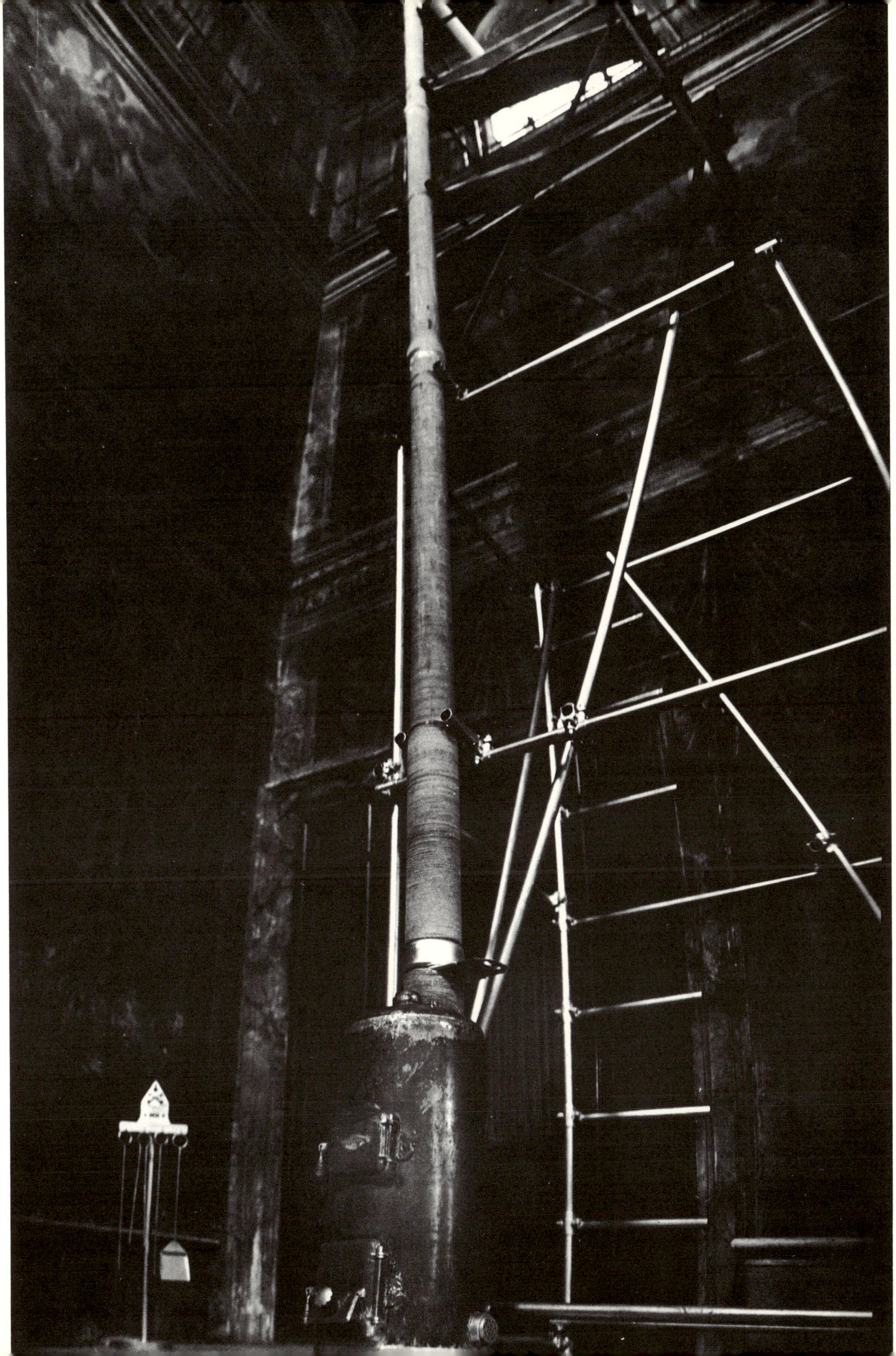

110   THE MAKING OF THE POPE

October 26, 27, and 28, 1958, those days on which the world watched and waited eagerly for the word that a new Pope had been elected. Unlike a political convention, where the deliberations, the political trading, and the backstage maneuvering are clearly visible to a watching public, in the election of the Pope everything is conducted with the most seemly and deliberate secrecy. There must be no record of doubt and uncertainty, of change of mind and heart, of suggestion of compromise. This is as it should be, for the Papacy ought to be free of the record or memory of politics, and the wise rule by which all trace of dissension in the Sacred College goes up the chimney in a wisp of smoke has assured that each new Pope will come to office with the unity of the Senate of the Church assured him.

Yet, of course, the period of three days of inconclusive balloting tells its own story with eloquence. Two decades before, upon the death of Pope Pius XI, Eugenio

The conclave was saddened by the death of Cardinal Mooney just before the sessions were scheduled to begin.

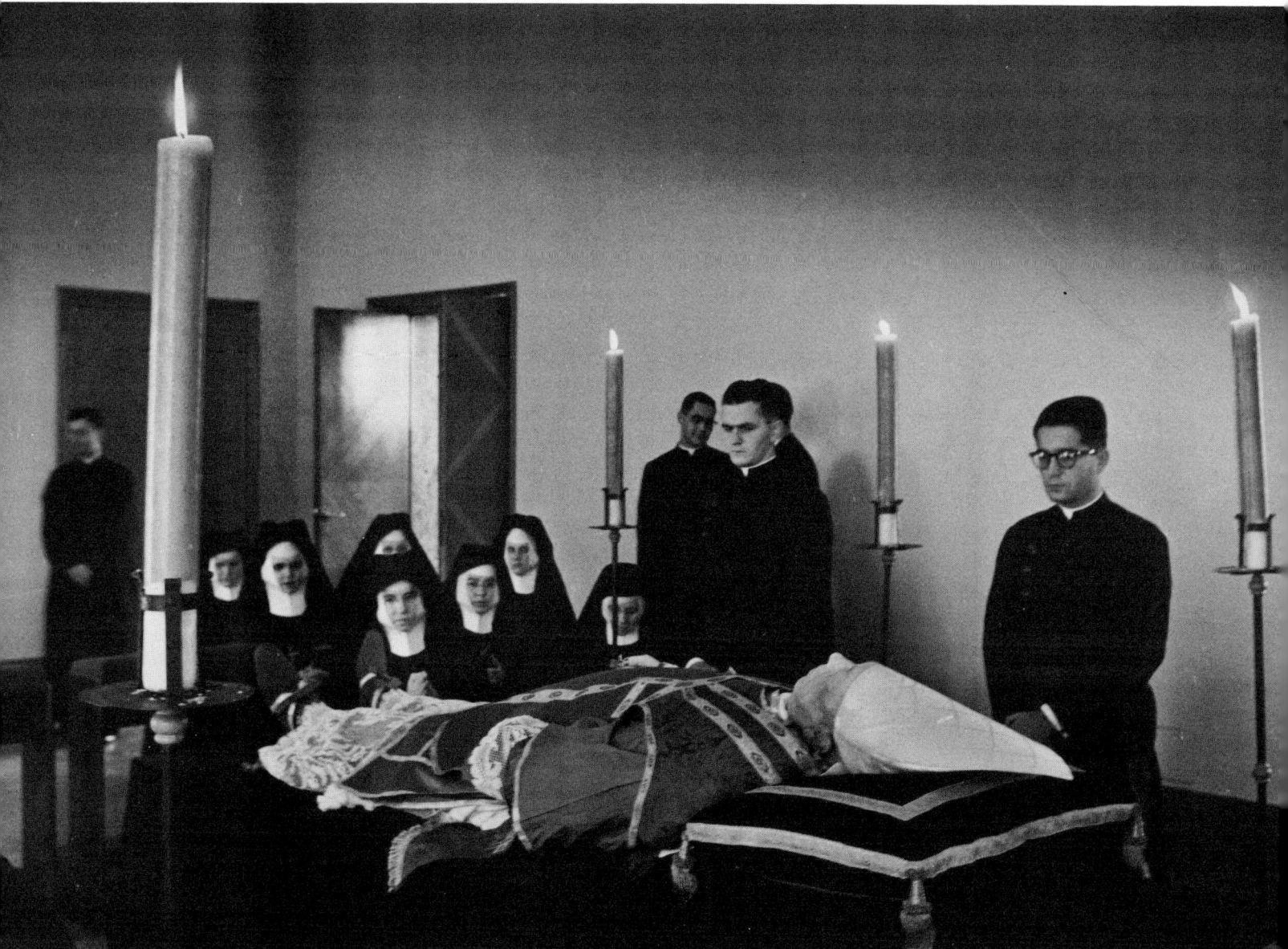

ORARIO

ore 9 - Messa dello Spirito Santo nella Cappella Sistina.

ore 13 - Pranzo.

ore 16 - Riunione degli Eminentissimi Sig. Cardinali nella Cappella Sistina.

ore 16,15 - I Conclavisti si recheranno nella Cappella Matilde per la recita del Santo Rosario.

ore 20,30 - Cena.

IL SEGRETARIO DEL CONCLAVE

Each day's schedule was given to the conclavists by the secretary.

The Borgia Apartment in the Vatican Palace served as the conclave dining room.

Seating arrangements: Diagram of the Sistine Chapel with official seating plan for the balloting. (Note arrow indicating absence of Cardinal Mindszenty.)

ACTA
APOSTOLICAE SEDIS

COMMENTARIUM OFFICIALE

Annus XXXVIII - Series II - Vol. XIII

TYPIS POLYGLOTTIS VATICANIS
M · DCCCC · XLVI

Title page of the *Acta Apostolicae Sedis*, the "Constitution" issued by Pope Pius XII to govern the election of his successor.

Pacelli had been clearly the outstanding candidate for succession, and his election seemed assured even before the Sacred College met. But when he died in 1958, there was no clear successor. There were many cardinals with the necessary qualifications who were held in sufficiently high regard by their colleagues to make them possible choices. But it became clear as the balloting proceeded that none was able to wrest the necessary two-thirds plus one of the ballots, and the talk of a compromise candidate began to be heard outside the sealed walls of the Palace.

When the election of Angelo Giuseppe Roncalli was announced many accepted his election as a compromise. His advanced age made it seem clear that the electors had chosen a "caretaker" Pope, who would rule briefly until a strong candidate could emerge. Yet seldom has the mystery of God's ways become more clearly apparent than in this. For Pope John XXIII has emerged as a strong and beloved Pope, with the mind, the heart, and the energy of a younger Pontiff, and with a vision that seems sure to make his Pontificate one of the great epochs of the Catholic Church. He has brought the Papacy close to the people, he has analyzed the heart of the problems of the modern Church, and he has in his wisdom called a council that is certain to take its place among the great ecumenical councils of Church history.

And so we can regard with awe the working of a Divine hand that guided the conclave of 1958 to its historic decision, and gave the Church reason for rejoicing over the outcome of that fateful election.

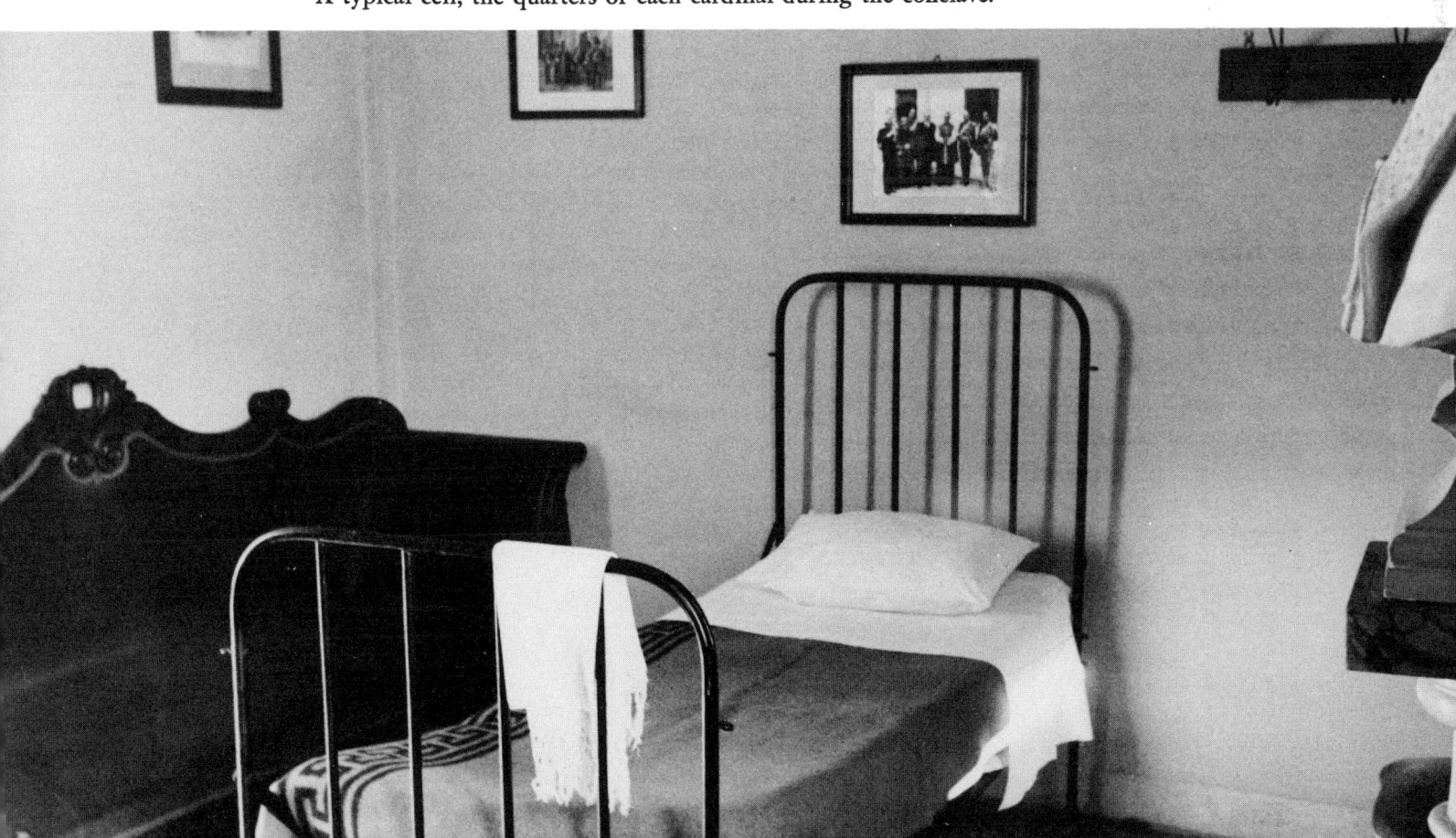

A typical cell, the quarters of each cardinal during the conclave.

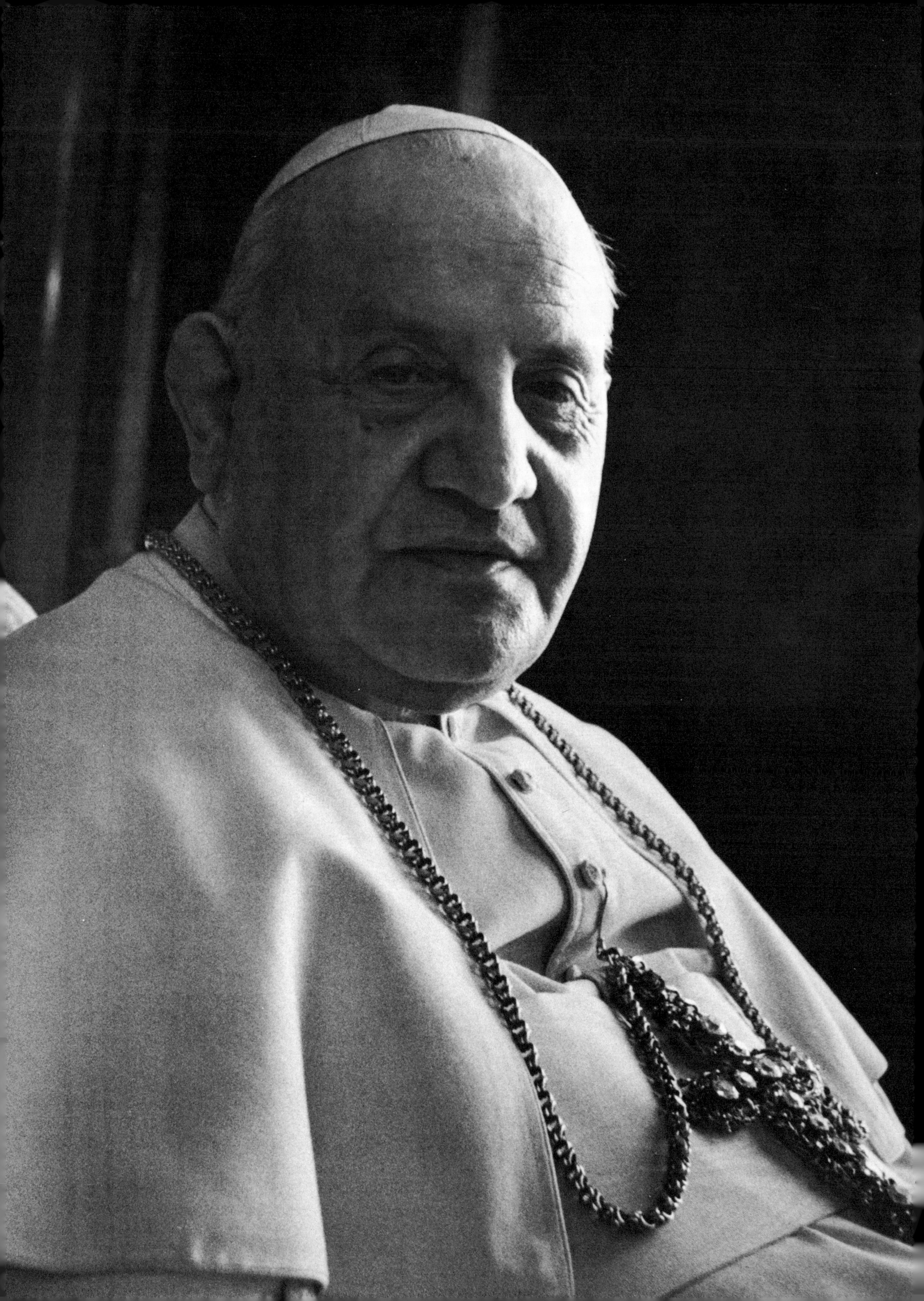

The Pontificate of Pope John XXIII

"Acceptasne electionem de Te canonice factam in Romanum Pontificem?"

With these words, spoken in ancient Latin, Cardinal Tisserant, Dean of the Sacred College of Cardinals, asked Angelo Giuseppe Roncalli, Patriarch of Venice, if he would accept the office just conferred upon him of Supreme Pontiff of the Roman Catholic Church.

"Accepto," Cardinal Roncalli replied, and the Church had a new Pope. With that simple word the keys of the Kingdom of Heaven passed into his keeping, as they had passed from Pope to Pope for nearly two thousand years, since our Savior entrusted them to his disciple Peter.

Four years have passed since Pope John XXIII ascended the Papal throne, long enough to evaluate his public utterances and his acts as Supreme Pontiff. That he would not be a passive Pope became evident almost immediately, for the day after his election he delivered a masterful public address. One can not better begin to assess his Pontificate than to weigh the words of his inspiring first address:

"In this anxious hour, We first address Our prayers to God. May He deign to strengthen Us in Our weakness and frailty, to enlighten Our mind, to direct Our will. For Our Predecessor of immortal memory, Pius XII, to whom the Catholic Church owes so much, is dead, and a Provident God has in accord with His mysterious designs laid on Us the burden of this Supreme Pontificate, which weighs heavily on our heart and almost crushes it.

"Next We greet with affection Our sons of the Sacred College of Cardinals, whose spiritual gifts and virtues are well known to Us. In particular We greet those who are unfortunately far from Us and whose sufferings and hardships trouble Us deeply.

"We wish also to express Our fatherly good will and affection for all Our venerable brothers in the episcopacy, who are tireless in their efforts to cultivate the Lord's vineyard throughout the world. And there are others whom We must mention: the priests, dispensers of God's mysteries, and especially the missionary priests, heralds of the divine word, who expend every effort to bring the truth of the Gos-

Pope John XXIII in repose beside the beautiful tapestry behind his desk in his study.

pel to far-off lands; the religious men and women, who are so zealously accomplishing great things; those who serve under the captaincy of the bishops in the peaceful militia of Catholic Action; and all others who assist in any way in the apostolate of the hierarchy. With deep affection We bless each and every one of these.

"Finally for all Our children in Christ, especially those who suffer from poverty or any sort of sorrow, We pray and beseech God in His goodness to grant each

Pope John XXIII in a typical gesture.

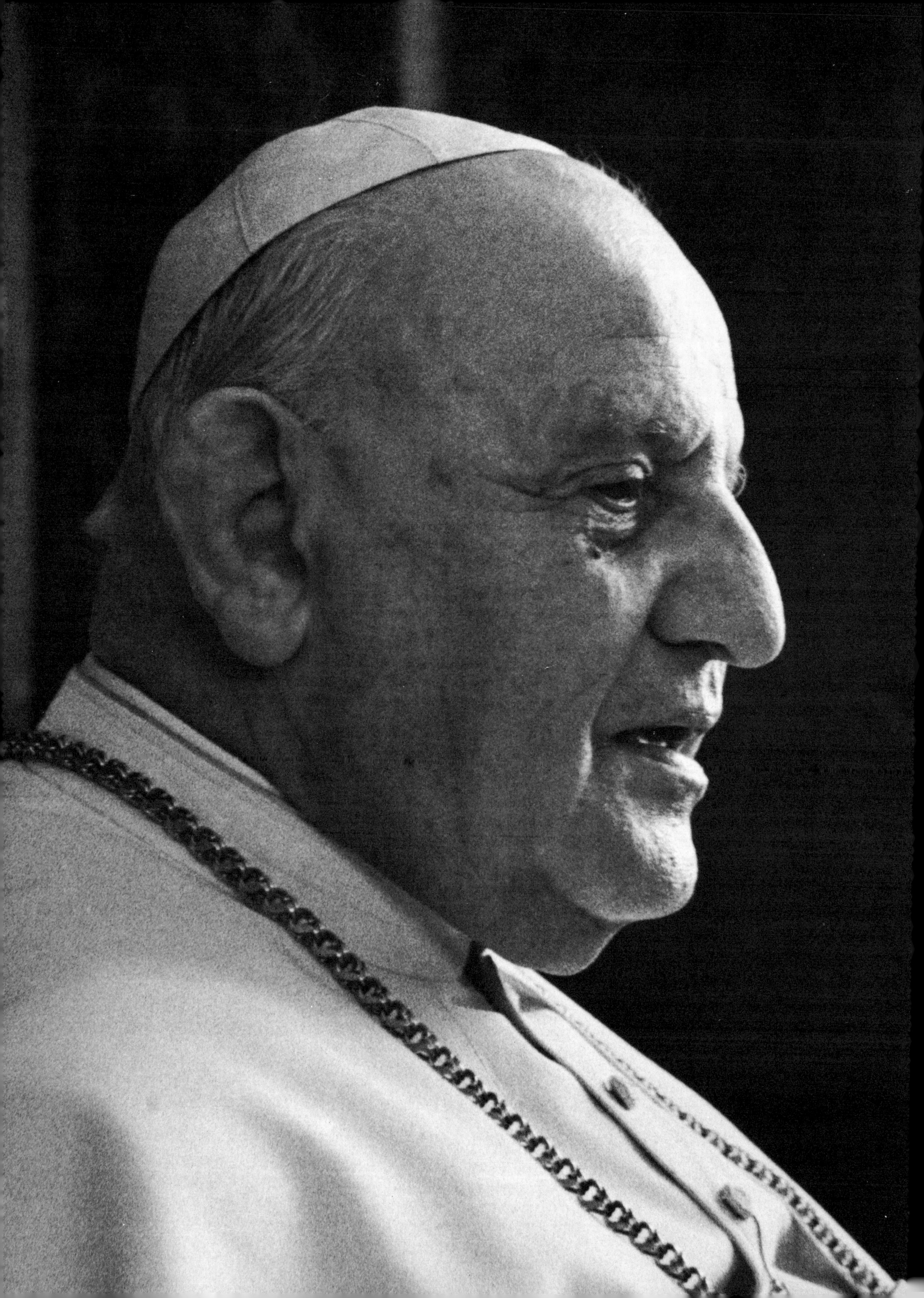

and every one of them in abundance the help and divine consolation they need.

"Among these children of Ours, those are particularly dear to Our paternal heart who live in the region of Venice, where We have exercised the pastoral ministry, and in the diocese of Bergamo, where We first saw the light of this mortal life. Although We are now far from them, We always are and always will be with them in the love of Jesus Christ. We are confident that their prayers will rise to God with Ours and win many heavenly graces.

"And now Our thoughts turn in a special way to the bishops, priests, religious and faithful who dwell in those lands where the Catholic Church is not given, or is not given fully, the freedom she deserves, where the rights of the Church are trampled under foot with reckless daring, where her lawful pastors are exiled or held in custody or so impeded that they can not perform their duties with due freedom. We want them all to know that We share their sorrows, their hardships and their sufferings, and We pray that God, the Giver of all good things, may soon put an end to these cruel persecutions, which are inconsistent not only with international peace and prosperity but with civilization itself and the basic right of man.

"May God pour forth His divine light into the minds of those who rule these nations. May He pardon the persecutors. May He grant better and happier days, in which all will enjoy the blessings of true liberty.

"We embrace the whole Church, Western and Eastern, with warm fatherly love. We open Our loving heart and extend Our outstretched arms to all who are separated from this Apostolic See, where Peter lives in his Successors 'even to the consummation of the world' (Matt. 28, 20) and fulfills Christ's command to bind and loose on earth (cf. Matt. 16, 19) and to feed the Lord's entire flock. (cf. John 21, 15-17)

"We long for their return to the house of the common Father and repeat the words of the Divine Redeemer: 'Holy Father, keep in thy name those whom thou hast given me, that they may be one even as we are.' (John 17, 11) For thus 'there shall be one fold and one shepherd.' (John 10, 16) We pray that they may all return freely and gladly; may this come to pass soon through the inspiration and assistance of God's grace. They will not find it a strange house but one that is truly their own, a house which has from time immemorial been enlightened by the teachings and adorned by the virtues of their forefathers.

"Now, however, We would like to address the rulers of all nations, men into whose hands have been placed the lot, fortune and hopes of their people. Why do they not settle their differences and disputes at last on an impartial basis? Why are the powers of human ingenuity and material resources so often directed to the production of weapons—grim instruments of death and destruction—rather than to the advance of prosperity among the various classes of citizens, especially among those who live in want?

A remarkable camera study of the Pope in a reflective mood.

"We know that great and complex difficulties stand in the way of realizing this worthy objective and settling these disagreements, but they must be surmounted and overcome, for this is a most serious matter and a serious goal intimately involved with the happiness of the whole human race.

"Take action then, boldly and with confidence. Heavenly light will shine upon you; God's help will be granted you. Look at the people who are entrusted to you! Listen to them! What do they want? What do they ask of you? Not for the new weapons our age has begotten for fratricide and general slaughter! But for peace, in which the human family may live, thrive and prosper freely; for justice, by which the classes can adjust equitably their mutual rights and duties; for tranquility and harmony, from which genuine prosperity arises.

"For in peace based on lawful individual rights and fostered by brotherly love the finest arts thrive, talents merge into virtue, public and private resources grow. You know what great men of the past have said on this topic: 'Peace is the ordered harmony of men.' (St. Augustine, *De Civitate Dei*, XIX, ch. 13) 'Peace is the tranquility of order.' (cf. ibid., and *Summa Theologica* II-II, 29, 1 ad 1) 'The name of peace is sweet and peace itself is a blessing, but there is a great deal of difference between peace and slavery. Peace is tranquil liberty.' (Cicero, 2nd *Philippic*, 44)

"We must ponder and consider with care the words the angels sang as they hovered over the Divine Infant's crib: 'Glory to God in the highest and on earth peace to men of good will.' (Luke 2, 14) But there is no real peace among men, peoples or nations unless peace has first been implanted in the hearts of individuals. There can be no outward peace unless it reflects and is ruled by that interior peace without which the affairs of men shake, totter and fall. And only God's holy religion can foster, strengthen and maintain such a peace.

"Let all take note of these facts who scorn God's name, trample on His holy rights and boldly endeavor to withdraw men from worship of Him!

"At this somber moment We repeat Our Divine Redeemer's words of promise: 'Peace I leave with you; my peace I give you.' (John 14, 27)

"May the Apostolic Blessing which We impart with fervent love upon the City and the World betoken and win this real peace as well as other heavenly gifts.

"But over and beyond external activity, it is important to know the spirit and the policies with which things are done. No doubt a Sovereign Pontificate takes its character from the Pontiff who conducts it and imparts a particular personality to it. But it is evident that the countenances of all the Roman Pontiffs who have through the centuries succeeded to the height of Apostolic Power have reflected or should have reflected the countenance of Jesus Christ, the Divine Master, who undertook his earthly journeys in order that he might sow the seed of divine learning and shed the light of good example.

"Of these divine teachings, certain words of the Gospel are the central point and precept which comprehends and embraces in itself all the others: 'Learn from me, for I am meek and humble of heart.' (Matt. 11, 29) This is the great principle of gentleness and humility. All of you throughout the world who are devout and 'fervent of spirit' (Rom. 12, 11) should pray assiduously to God for your Pontiff, with this intention: that he may advance more and more in the gentleness and humility of the Gospel. We are convinced that many benefits will follow from the exercise of these virtues, and if they become the customary manner of the Father of all the faithful, important advantages will result even by way of those human needs which pertain to the social and terrestrial order.

"Finally, Venerable Brothers, Cardinals and Bishops of the Holy Catholic Church, and beloved sons, priests and members of the faithful, We are pleased to direct your attention to a circumstance that gives Us great pleasure: the fact that this celebration falls upon a day which has a joyful meaning for Us as a priest and as a bishop. On this feastday, November fourth, on which the coronation of a new Sovereign Pontiff will henceforth be commemorated, the Universal Church celebrates each year in her sacred liturgy the feast of Saint Charles Borromeo. We have long had a special affection for this Bishop of Milan who must be numbered among the greatest shepherds of the flock. For it was thirty-four years ago that We were consecrated an Archbishop, amid solemn ecclesiastical services, in the church dedicated at Rome to his honor, where his heart is kept as a precious relic.

"You know that God's Church has at times amid the trials of the centuries lost some of her vigor but she has always found new strength again. It was in such a period of ecclesiastical decline that Saint Charles was called in the wisdom of a Provident God to the high task of restoration. Since he labored with might and main that the decrees of the Council of Trent might have the greatest possible efficacy and strove by his example to enforce them in Milan and throughout Italy, he well deserves the distinguished title 'Master of Bishops.' Sovereign Pontiffs took counsel of him; he was to a marvelous degree a model of episcopal holiness.

"During the religious services which accompany the coronation of a Sovereign Pontiff, it is permissible to add to the litanies the names of those Saints for whom the new Pope has a special devotion. And so when the invocation 'Saint Charles help him' was raised today, you prayed fervently, We are sure, that heavenly blessings might descend upon Us in abundance through the intercession of Saint Charles, Our patron, on whose support We rely now and in the future. Amen."

With this eloquent appeal for peace and godliness Pope John XXIII began his Pontificate. The new Pope had come to his high office from a long and dedicated service in the Church. Nearing his seventy-seventh birthday as he assumed the duties of the Papacy, he could look back on a career that had taken him far beyond the borders of his native Italy in the service of his Predecessors and that had earned him the greatest honors in the Church.

In northern Italy, near Milan, in the shadow of the mountains, lies the little village of Brusico, in the diocese of Bergamo, a typical Italian hill-town. Today the village has about two thousand inhabitants, and it was even tinier on November

25, 1881, when a third child and first son was born to Giovanni Battista Roncalli and his wife Marianna. Angelo grew up as one of ten children "in an atmosphere of self-sufficient blessed poverty," helping his father and his brothers, wrest a bare existence out of the ancient soil.

The Roncallis were a hardy people. Giovanni was eighty-one when he died in 1935 and his wife Marianna was eighty-four when she died in 1939. They had lived to see their firstborn son rise to a high position in the Church, and both devoutly religious, they took great joy in his high clerical honors. Three of the Pope's brothers are still living, and one sister, and he has fourteen nieces and nephews. Two of his brothers still live in the old farmhouse and still work the family acres.

Angelo's first education was in the rustic local one-room school, but his thirst for learning was evident from earliest childhood. By the time he was eleven, he had already decided to become a priest, and he entered the diocesan seminary at Bergamo, where he remained as a student for eight years. He is remembered in the records there as a youth of strong character, notable intelligence and humility, but imbued with self-confidence and an evident desire to succeed.

Upon his graduation with honors at the age of nineteen, the young man was chosen for advanced study in theology at the Collegio Ceresoli in Rome, where he came under the spiritual influence of the eminent director, Father Francesco Pitocchi. In his studies at the Collegio, he gave further clear evidence of his superior ability, and after four years of study he received his doctorate, having taken the written examination on a theme selected by Eugenio Pacelli, who as Pope Pius XII was the immediate predecessor of Pope John XXIII.

On August 10, 1904, in the Church of Santa Maria in Rome, Angelo Roncalli was ordained a priest by Bishop Ceppetelli, Vicar of Rome. The young priest was twenty-three, and the day after he was ordained he had the great joy of being able to celebrate his first Mass at the tomb of St. Peter, in the great basilica. Here he met the new Pope, Pius X, and received the Pope's blessing.

A few months later young Father Roncalli had a fortuitous experience that was destined to have a great influence on his career. Just a few weeks after his twenty-fourth birthday, he attended the ceremonies at Rome in which several new bishops were consecrated. Among them was Bishop Radini-Tedeschi, descendent of a noble family of Piacenza, who had just been assigned to the diocese of Bergamo. He needed as a secretary a priest familiar with the diocese to which he was going, and upon recommendation of the director of the seminary, he chose Father Roncalli for this important post. The new Bishop was an important man in the Church hierarchy and a leader in the new Catholic social action movement, and the nine years that Father Roncalli spent with him gave the young priest much practical experience in dealing with the problems of the Church on a diocesan level. He was able to pursue his studies extensively, and he spent much time in the Ambrosian Library in Milan. He also spent the greater part of these nine years teaching ecclesiastical history at the seminary of Bergamo, where his students later recalled him as a gentle, persuasive, and above all always interesting teacher.

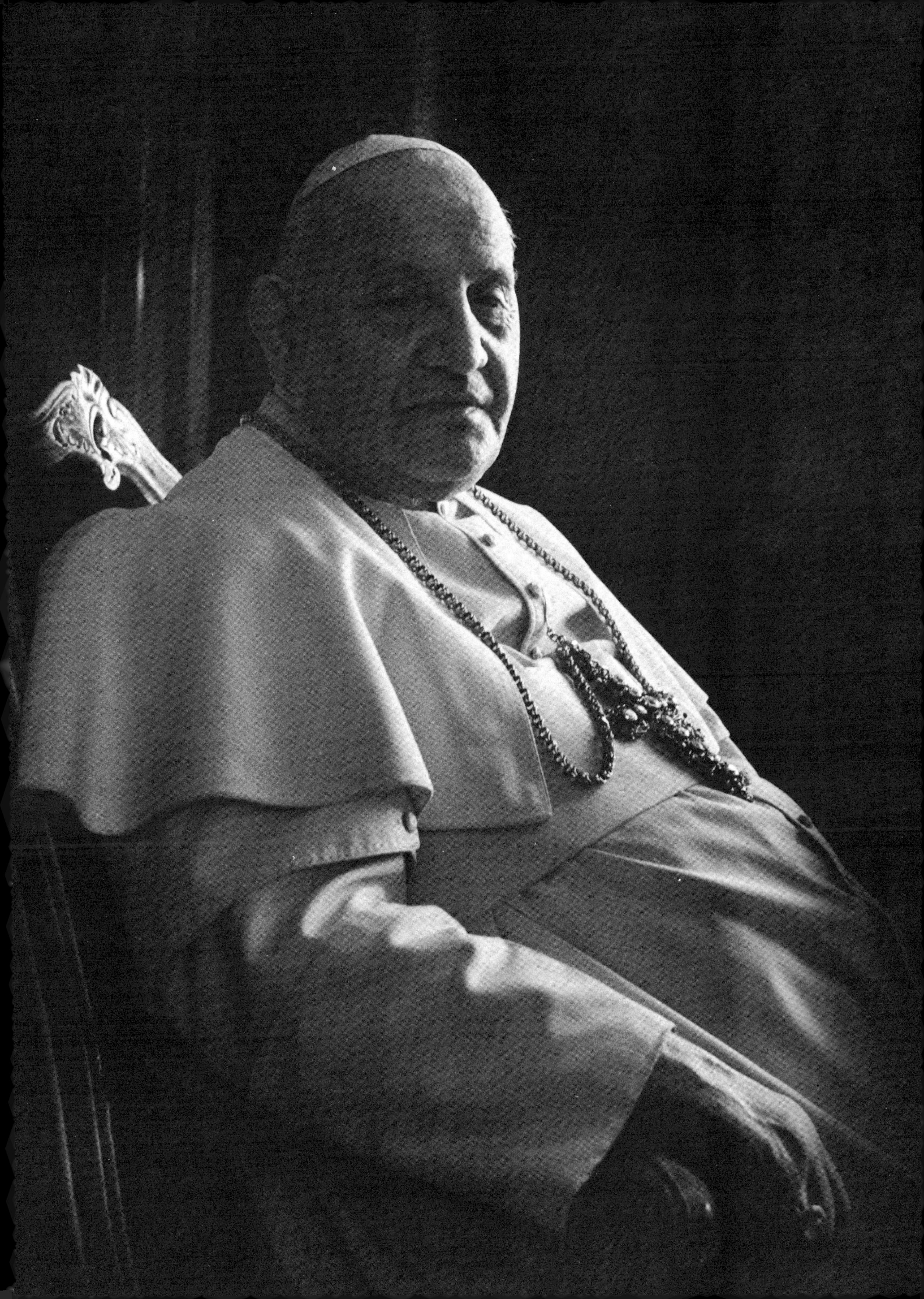

Bishop Radini-Tedeschi traveled extensively during these years, and his secretary accompanied him to Spain, France and Palestine, wonderful experiences for a young country priest. Upon the death of the Bishop in 1914, the association came to an end. Father Roncalli had been working on a book on the life of his patron saint, St. Charles Borromeo, and when he published it, he dedicated the book to the memory of the Bishop, in whose service he had spent the formative years of his career.

But now Father Roncalli was called to a greater service. World War I had plunged most of Europe into chaos, and when Italy entered the war a few months later, many young priests were called into military service. Father Roncalli had served briefly in the army after his graduation from the seminary, and now he entered the army as a chaplain with the rank of lieutenant. He served with distinction in several hospitals in northern Italy, and he later recalled that his war service had added much to his understnding of the human soul.

With the end of the war, Father Roncalli returned to Bergamo, where he plunged into a project that had long been forming in his mind. In the Palazzo Asperti he established a house where poor young students could live and work in comfort in a spiritual atmosphere, and he had the satisfaction of seeing his project become so successful that similar houses were established in many parts of Italy.

Bishop Marelli had succeeded to the diocese of Bergamo, and he appointed Father Roncalli to be spiritual director of the seminary.

His outstanding work soon brought him to the attention of the Vatican, and in 1921, in his fortieth year, Father Roncalli was summoned to Rome by Pope Benedict XV, who had selected him for an important task. He was raised to the rank and title of Monsignor, and was appointed to head the National Committee for the Propagation of the Faith. In his work with this committee he found it necessary to visit many regions of Italy and to travel to Paris, Brussels, Munich, and other European cities.

By 1925 another Pope sat on the throne of St. Peter, and Monsignor Roncalli ascended another step in the hierarchy. He was consecrated a bishop with the title of Titular Archbishop of Areopolis. On the occasion of his consecration, *Osservatore Romano* characterized him as a man of "sound piety, rare intelligence, formidable learning, ardent zeal and a fine sense of judgment."

He was entrusted with a most important mission, as Apostolic Visitator to Bulgaria, where the Roman Catholic Church was in a most difficult position. The Orthodox Church was recognized as the official state religion, and had six million adherents, while the Roman Catholic Church had only the barest foothold, with about forty-five thousand members, and these divided into two rites. Archbishop Roncalli threw himself into his now work with his usual thoroughness, and on the occasion of his second Christmas in Bulgaria, he was able to deliver a part of his Christmas sermon in the Bulgarian language. He introduced a new vitality into the Catholic community, brought about extensive improvement in Catholic education, solved the difficult problems relating to marriages between members of the Orthodox and Catholic faiths, and in all served a decade in this post with energy and distinction.

In Bulgaria, Archbishop Roncalli was able to see and understand the problems relating to the division of the Catholic Church. Here the Oriental Rite was side by side with the Latin Church. Because of his experiences here he was able to bring to the Papacy a sound understanding of the Eastern Church.

By the end of 1934, the Archbishop was given a new and even more important mission. He was named Apostolic Delegate to Greece and Turkey and administrator of the vicariate of Constantinople. This was a mission to test all of the diplomacy and tact of which Archbishop Roncalli was capable, for in Greece, as a representative of the Pope, he was accorded no official recognition, and in Turkey, where Catholics were in a tiny minority, he encountered great official hostility toward all things Christian. It is a great tribute to his ability as a diplomat that he was able to carry out his mission with such success that upon his elevation to the Papacy, Greek newspapers were able to remember his work in Greece with high praise and genuine affection. In Turkey, he tried to avoid any contact with the temporal government, emphasizing the purely spiritual aspects of his mission. He studied Turkish history, language and traditions, and made himself a popular and respected administrator.

This mission lasted also a decade. By 1944, a new Pope once again occupied the Vatican, the wise and capable Pacelli, Pope Pius XII. A most difficult situation had arisen with respect to the position of the Church in France. In 1940, with the fall of France, Archbishop Valerio Valeri had accompanied the occupation government of Marshal Petain to Vichy. By the end of 1944 there could be no doubt of the outcome of the war, and with the return of a legitimate government to Paris, the position of a Papal nuncio who had been attached to the Petain government would be embarrassing to the Vatican. Here the Vatican needed a man of keen judgment and a perfect gift for diplomacy. The choice fell upon Archbishop Roncalli.

The mission to France was the greatest test of Roncalli's ability. The new French government viewed the Vatican with distrust and hostility, but the nunciature of Roncalli was successful in bringing about a reconciliation that enabled the Church to emerge united and independent of state control.

On January 12, 1953, another turning point came in the life of the Archbishop. He was already seventy-one years old and he had spent a long and honored life in the service of the Church. At a time when most men have already retired from active life, and are content to bask in the sunset of human existence, this amazing man was about to enter upon a new phase of his career. On that date, in a secret consistory in Rome, Pius XII raised his nuncio to the rank of Cardinal, and the President of France, Vincent Auriol, conferred on him his scarlet Cardinal's biretta.

At the same time fresh news came from Rome. Cardinal Roncalli, the Vatican's leading diplomat, was to become again a pastor, with his appointment as the Patriarch and Bishop of the ancient city of Venice. To Cardinal Roncalli, who had always felt his true vocation to be that of pastor of the flock and teacher, this was welcome news indeed, and he looked forward to his return to Italy after nearly three decades of service abroad.

How his heart must have leaped at his reception in Venice. Even this city, with centuries of pomp and ceremony in its history, outdid itself. Almost the entire populace of Venice lined the Grand Canal, cheering the new Patriarch; the palaces were hung with rich damasks, brocades and bunting, and in the van of the Bishop's procession ended at the Cathedral of St. Mark, where the body of the great evangelist lies. Here, in his inaugural sermon, Cardinal Roncalli recalled that he was following in the footsteps of the great Pope Pius X, who had served as Bishop of Venice.

Despite his advanced age and a long career that would have exhausted most other men, Cardinal Roncalli entered upon his new duties with great zeal and enthusiasm. He personally visited the many parishes under his jurisdiction and met hundreds of his parishioners. He visited hospitals, schools and convents, led his people in programs of Catholic action, attended social and cultural meetings. Under his patriarchy, some thirty parish churches were erected, and a new minor seminary was built. In 1957 he presided over a diocesan synod to set forth new precepts for his clergy. Thus when Cardinal Roncalli went to Rome in October of 1958 to attend the conclave of Papal electors, he could look back on more than half a century of service in the Church as pastor, teacher, administrator, and diplomat.

As Pope John XXIII, Cardinal Roncalli assumed perhaps the most difficult and complex administrative position in the entire modern world. As the leader of one-fifth of the world's population in all matters spiritual, his is certainly the largest single administrative unit in the world. Few people, even Catholics have any conception of the scope and magnitude of the administrative problems that beset the Vatican.

As to the scope of the modern Papacy, the statistics give some idea of size: The Pope is the head of a worldwide administration comprising 87 cardinals, more than 300 metropolitan archbishops and resident archbishops, 1200 resident bishops, nearly 900 titular archbishops and bishops, 79 prelates and abbots, 12 apostolic administrators, 19 prelates of the Oriental Rite, more than 200 vicars apostolic, 122 prefects apostolic, 365,000 priests, 270,000 other male religious, about 1,000,000 nuns, and nearly 550,000,000 Church members. In the United States alone there are some 42,000,000 Catholics, 9,000,000 pupils under instruction in Catholic schools, 168,000 teachers. Administratively the United States has 26 archdioceses, 114 dioceses, 185 bishops, 43 abbots, and a total of nearly 55,000 priests.

To administer this tremendous spiritual network, the Catholic Church has a complex but well-defined governmental machinery. As we have already noted, the Sacred College of Cardinals serves as the legislative arm of the Catholic government, electing and advising the Popes.

Pope John standing beside his desk with a favorite tapestry behind him.

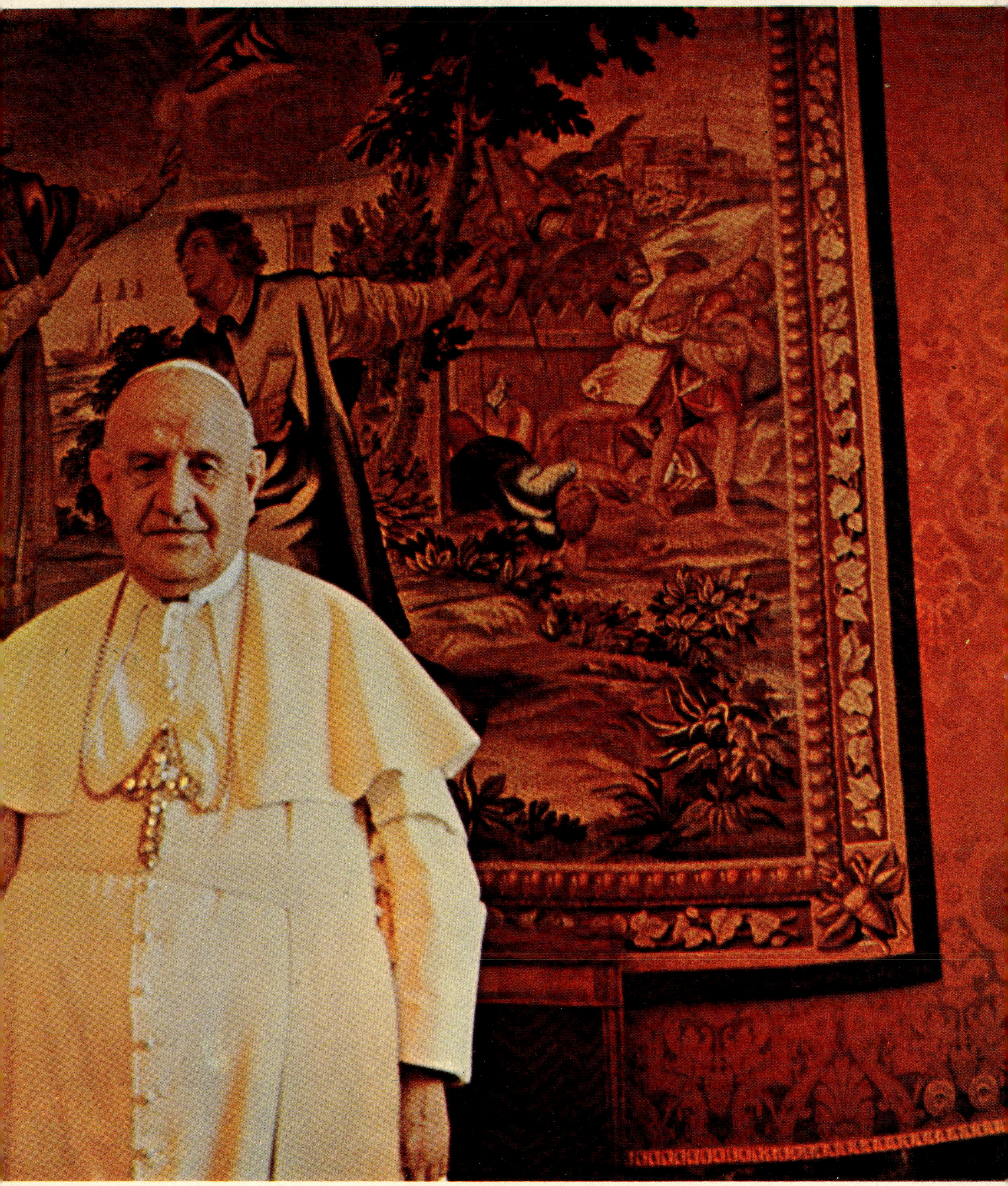

The "executive" arm is by far the largest and most complex. The Pope governs his far-flung constituency through twelve executive divisions or "congregations," the heads of which together make up the "cabinet." The Pope himself presides over three of these, the most important being the Sacred Congregation of the Holy Office, which is charged with matters of doctrine and morals. The Pope is also the prefect of the Sacred Consistorial Congregation, which relates to the administration of certain diocesan affairs. Under this heading come the establishment of new dioceses, provinces, and other administrative divisions, appointment of new resident bishops and reports from the various dioceses under its jurisdiction. The third congregation administered under the direction of the Pope himself is the Sacred Congregation for the Oriental Church, in which Pope John XXIII has such great personal interest.

The other congregations or administrative divisions are the Sacred Congregation of Sacraments, dealing with discipline of the seven sacraments; the Sacred Congregation of the Council, concerned with administration of Church property, the duties of pastors and observance of the precepts of Church discipline; the Sacred Congregation for Religious, dealing with the government, discipline, studies, property and prerogative of religious orders; the Sacred Congregation for the Propagation of the Faith, which has jurisdiction over all missionary organizations and activities; the Sacred Congregation of Rites, which governs in matters relating to Church ceremony, beatification and cannonization; the Sacred Congregation of Ceremonies deals with ceremonies to be observed in the Papal court and rules of protocol affecting cardinals and diplomatic representatives in the Vatican; the Sacred Congregation for Extraordinary Ecclesiastical Affairs, which may be likened to the Vatican's Department of State, dealing as it does with civil governments in matters relating to negotiation of concordats; the Sacred Congregation of Seminaries and Universities, which administers the affairs of colleges and universities not under the direction of missionary societies.

The Holy See also has its judicial system, consisting of three tribunals, the Sacred Penitentiary, the Sacred Roman Rota, and the Supreme Apostolic Signature. The Sacred Penitentiary acts in matters of conscience. It may receive petitions for absolution from sin and censure, and may grant dispensation from vows or oaths. Petitions may be brought to the Penitentiary directly or, as is most usual, through a priest, and the rescript or decision is usually presented sealed through the chosen confessor. The rescript may grant relief, or it may prescribe certain conditions of penance, which then become the responsibility of the confessor to administer.

The Sacred Roman Rota may be likened to a court of appeals. It hears cases involving judicial procedure. It has a specifically constituted panel of "judges" presided over by a dean.

The "supreme court" of the Catholic Church is the Supreme Apostolic Signature, consisting of seven cardinals, presided over by a prefect. It has final jurisdiction, except in cases pertaining to the Sacred Congregation of the Holy Office or the Sacred Congregation of Rites.

This then is the great government of which Pope John XXIII is the head and the guiding spirit. The modern world has not heretofore known such a Pope. He is warm, friendly, smiling—truly a Pope of the people. Reared in the strict protocol of the Church, he is nevertheless impatient of protocol. Already a great body of anecdotes is available to illustrate this. It is said that soon after his election, he called for his car one day to visit St. Paul's Outside the Wall, one of the great basilicas of Rome about two miles from the Vatican. What this would have involved may be indicated by quoting some of the terms of the Lateran Treaty. For outside the Vatican the Pope would have to be considered a visiting foreign chief of state. He must be assigned a police escort and accorded the full honors due a foreign potentate. That was one trip he did not make, but it is an open secret that the Pope has made many excursions outside the Vatican, visiting clerical friends, churches, hospitals, prisons. It is said that in the first four months of his reign he went outside the Vatican more than his predecessor did in the twenty years of his Pontificate.

The result of all this has been to create a new image of the Papacy. One effect of this has been to open the door of the Vatican to representatives of other churches and governments. Only a few months after Pope John ascended the Papal throne, he had a visit from the Greek Archbishop Iakovos, the first time in more than three centuries that a representative of the Orthodox Church had visited the Vatican. The King and Queen of Greece also visited the Pope, ending an unbroken precedent of five hundred years, and perhaps most startling of all to the world was the visit of the Archbishop of Canterbury, Geoffrey Fisher, the ruling prelate of the Church of England.

All this of course has had an understandable significance in view of Pope John's call for a council to meet in the Vatican in October, 1962. This is the second Vatican Council, the first having met in 1869. The deliberations of the first Vatican Council were interrupted by the coming of the Franco-Prussian War in 1870, and many of the topics that had been proposed for discussion were put aside. However, that council did declare for all time the infallibility of the Pope.

The call for the council of 1962 was issued by Pope John as one of the first great acts of his Pontificate, early in 1959. He allowed a period of three years for discussion of the topics that might properly come before the council and the formulation of ideas and arguments. The plans for the council have stirred worldwide interest, even outside of Catholic circles, for it is anticipated that one of the most important topics to be discussed will be the possible avenues by which dissident Christian churches may return to the Mother Church. This proposal has already brought forth strong reactions from many churchmen, ranging from the open interest of the German Lutherans to the skeptical position of some American Protestant groups. Whether any tangible plans in this direction will emerge from the council remains to be seen, but there is no doubt that after many centuries there is at last some progressive thinking in this direction.

There are many thorny problems in the way of Christian unity. Nevertheless, it

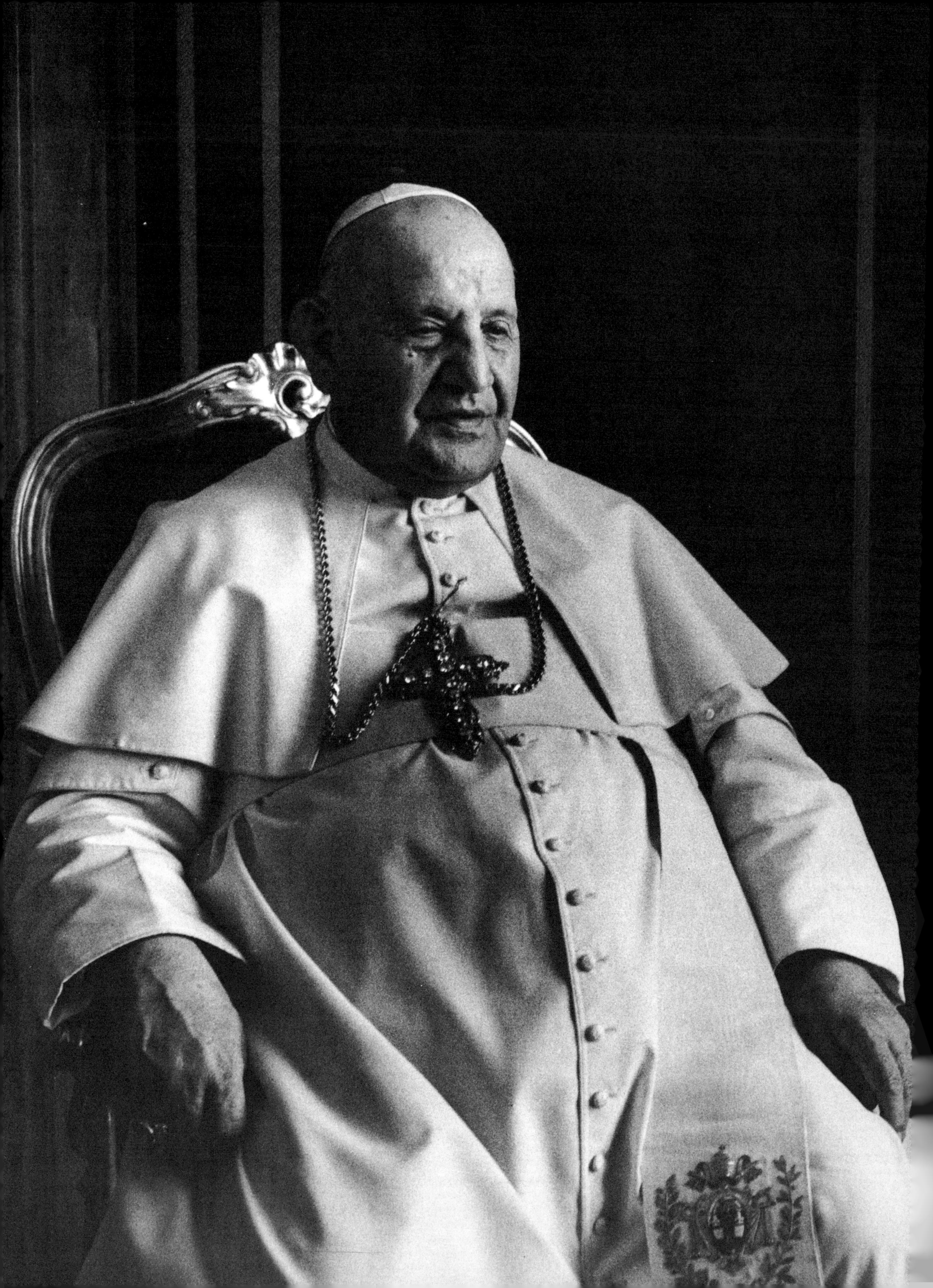

is confidently believed that the council will take up the question of Christian unity and set forth the means by which this may in time be accomplished.

The council is expected to act on a wide range of topics designed to clarify Church doctrine in a world that has altered greatly in the century since the last ecumenical council. There will undoubtedly be active discussion of some change in the liturgy to make it more understandable to members of the Church, and there will undoubtedly be strong argument in favor of wider use of vernacular language in place of the ancient Latin. There will be consideration of the position of Christian morals in an age in which medicine and psychology have made tremendous strides and in which new sociological points of view have become apparent. The council is expected also to deal with the Church's position with relation to the rise of Marxist, humanist, and existentialist philosophies.

But first and foremost, this will be the council of Pope John XXII. Already he has impressed his personality upon the affairs of the world. He has shown a keen perception of world problems and an eagerness to grapple with them. Thus it is not too much to hope that the council will provide new insight for our troubled times. From the earliest days of his Pontificate, Pope John has stressed his role as a teacher and an interpreter. In his five Encyclical Letters issued in his Pontificate he has shown those qualities of understanding and deep concern which have characterized his entire career.

The first Encyclical Letter of his reign was issued on June 29, 1959, just eight months after he became Pope. Discussing in broad terms the problems of the Church in the modern world, he set forth his views on Christian unity, peace, and truth. This letter is known under the title *Ad Petri Cathedram*. In his second letter, *Sacerdotii Nostri Primordia*, the Pope commends to the attention of all priests the exemplary life of St. John Vianney as a standard of the ministry. In his third letter, *Grata Recordatio*, he dealt with the prayer of the Rosary, and in *Princeps Pastorum*, his fourth letter, the Pope discussed the missionary work of the Church.

But it is the fifth Encyclical Letter, published on May 15, 1961, which has established before the world the tone of this Pontificate. *Mater et Magistra*, "Mother and Teacher," is a wise and noble document, rich in its understanding of the complex problems of the modern world. Ranging far in the maze of modern philosophy, economics, politics, and world affairs, the Pope discusses automation, atomic energy, social legislation, control of business cycles, wages, and full employment. He throws the weight of the Church on the side of individual rights and the protection of the family. He urges a greater share for the workers in the ownership, management and profits of industry.

Of greatest concern to the Pontiff in this historic document is the cause of world peace. Upholding the work of the United Nations organizations in several areas, he pleads for world co-operation to solve the modern problems of mankind. In the complex world of today, nations can no longer pursue their own interests in

Pope John XXIII.

isolation. He warns: "The different political communities can no longer adequately solve their major problems in their own surroundings and with their own forces, even though they be communities which are notable for their high level and diffusion of culture. For the number and industriousness of their citizens, for the efficiency of their economic systems and the vastness and richness of their territories, political communities react on each other. It may be said that each succeeds in development of itself by contributing to the development of the others."

He speaks with concern of the needs of the underdeveloped countries, and redressing the balance between the wealthy and the poor nations. "It is obvious that the solidarity of the human race and Christian brotherhood demand that an active and manifold co-operation be established among the peoples of the world. They demand a co-operation which permits and encourages the movement of goods, capital, and men with a view to eliminating or reducing the above-mentioned imbalance."

It is clear that in Pope John XXIII the world has found a grasp of issues, an understanding, a broad sympathy. The Second Vatican Council is not only a council of the Catholic Church. Observers representing many faiths and many nations will be present, weighing the words and the actions of the assembled Churchmen. The voice of Pope John XXIII will be heard, and it is a voice that speaks with sympathetic concern for the needs of a troubled world. It is a voice that spreads optimism and understanding and above all hope—hope for a world much in need of hope for a brighter tomorrow.

Highlights of the Life of Angelo Giuseppe Roncalli

November 25, 1881—Born, the third child of Giovanni Battista Roncalli and his wife, Mariana Mazzola at Sotto il Monte in the province of Bergamo, Italy.

1892–1900—In studies at the seminary of Bergamo.

August 4, 1903—Election of Giuseppe Sarto, Pope Pius X.

1900–1904—In advanced studies in Theology at the Papal Seminary in Rome.

August 10, 1904—After obtaining a doctorate in Theology at the Papal Seminary, ordained a priest.

1905–1914—Private secretary and assistant to the Bishop of Bergamo. Also, teacher in Theology and Ecclesiastical history at the seminary at Bergamo.

1908—Published *Records of the Apostolic Visitation of Carlo Borromeo to Bergamo in 1575*.

September 4, 1914—Election of Giacomo Della Chiesa, as Pope Benedict XV.

1915—In military service as medical orderly and Chaplain in hospitals.

1916—Published *The Life of Monsignor Radini-Tedeschi, Bishop of Bergamo*.

1921—Assigned to the Congregation of Propaganda in Rome by Pope Benedict XV.

1922—Achille Ratti became Pope Pius XI on death of Pope Benedict XV (March 19).

1923—Made Honorary Canon of Bergamo and Domestic Prelate.

1925—Ordained Bishop and named Apostolic Visitor to Bulgaria by Pope Pius XI.

1930—Named Apostolic Delegate to Bulgaria.

1935–1944—Apostolic Delegate to Turkey.

1939—Death of Pope Pius XI (February 10) and election of Eugenio Pacelli, Pope Pius XII.

1944—Named Papal Nuncio to Paris by Pope Pius XII.

1952—Awarded the Grande Croix of the Legion d'Honneur by the French Government in recognition of his efforts in behalf of peace in Europe.

1953—Created Cardinal by Pope Pius XII at a Consistory (January 12) and three days later became Patriarch and Archbishop of Venice. Cardinal Roncalli's red hat was conferred upon him by President M. Vincent Auriol of France.

1953-1958—Patriarch and Archbishop of Venice.

1958—Elected Pope of the Roman Catholic Church (October 28) and assumed the name of John the Twenty-Third. November 4, 1958, coronation as Pope.

January 25, 1959—Announced plans to hold 21st Ecumenical Council at Rome.

June 29, 1959—Issued encyclical letter *Ad Petri Cathedram*.

August 1, 1959—Issued encyclical letter *Sacerdotii Nostri Primordia*

September 26, 1959—Issued encyclical *Grata Recordatio*.

November 28, 1959—Issued encyclical *Princeps Pastorum*.

May 15, 1961—Issued encyclical *Mater et Magistra*.

February 2, 1962—Set October 11, 1962 as date for the opening of the Roman Catholic Church's first ecumenical council in nearly 100 years.

March 19, 1962—Held a consistory which named ten new Cardinals and increased the total number of members of the College of Cardinals to eighty-seven, the highest number in the history of the Roman Catholic Church.

October 11, 1962—Opening of the second Vatican Council at Rome.

Previous Ecumenical Councils

Listed by places and dates (A.D.).

1. 1 Nicaea, 325
2. 1 Constantinople, 381
3. Ephesus, 431
4. Chalcedon, 451
5. 2 Constantinople, 553
6. 3 Constantinople, 680–81
7. 2 Nicaea, 787
8. 4 Constantinople, 869
9. 1 Lateran (Rome), 1123
10. 2 Lateran, 1139
11. 3 Lateran, 1179
12. 4 Lateran, 1215
13. 1 Lyons, 1245
14. 2 Lyons, 1274
15. Vienne, 1311–12
16. Constance, 1414–18
17. Basel and Ferrara-Florence, 1431–1445
18. 5 Lateran, 1512–17
19. Trent, 1545–63
20. Vatican, 1869–70

List of Popes

St. Peter, d. 67?
St. Linus, 67–76?
St. Cletus, 76?–88?
St. Clement I, 88?–97?
St. Evaristus, 97?–105?
St. Alexander I, 105?–115?
St. Sixtus I, 115?–125?
St. Telesphorus, 125?–136?
St. Hyginus, 136?–140?
St. Pius I, 140?–155?
St. Anicetus, 155?–166?
St. Soter, 166?–175?
St. Eleutherius, 175?–189?
St. Victor I, 189–199
St. Zephyrinus, 199–217
St. Calixtus I, 217–22
St. Urban I, 222–30
St. Pontian, 230–35
St. Anterus, 235–36
St. Fabian, 236–50
St. Cornelius, 251–53
St. Lucius I, 253–54
St. Stephen I, 254–57
St. Sixtus II, 257–58
St. Dionysius, 259–68
St. Felix I, 269–74
St. Eutychian, 275–83
St. Caius, 283–96
St. Marcellinus, 296–304
St. Marcellus I, 308–9
St. Eusebius, 309 or 310
St. Miltiades, 311–14
St. Sylvester I, 314–35
St. Marcus, 336
St. Julius I, 337–52
Liberius, 352–66
St. Damasus I, 366–84
St. Siricius, 384–99
St. Anastasius I, 399–401
St. Innocent I, 401–17
St. Zosimus 417–18
St. Boniface I, 418–22
St. Celestine I, 422–32

St. Sixtus III, 432–40
St. Leo I, 440–61
St. Hilary, 461–68
St. Simplicius, 468–83
St. Felix III (II), 483–92
St. Gelasius I, 492–96
Anastasius II, 496–98
St. Symmachus, 498–514
St. Hormisdas, 514–23
St. John I, 523–26
St. Felix IV (III), 526–30
Boniface II, 530–32
John II, 533–35
St. Agapetus I, 535–36
St. Silverius, 536–37
Vigilius, 537–55
Pelagius I, 556–61
John III, 561–74
Benedict I, 575–79
Pelagius II, 579–90
St. Gregory I, 590–604
Sabinianus, 604–6
Boniface III, 607
St. Boniface IV, 608–15
St. Deusdedit I, 615–18
Boniface V, 619–25
Honorius I, 625–38
Severinus, 640
John IV, 640–42
Theodore I, 642–49
St. Martin I, 649–55
St. Eugene I, 654–57
St. Vitalian, 657–72
Adeodatus II, 672–76
Donus, 676–78
St. Agathon, 678–81
St. Leo II, 682–83
St. Benedict II, 684–85
John V, 685–86
Conon, 686–87
St. Sergius I, 687–701
John VI, 701–5
John VII, 705–7

Sisinnius, 708
Constantine, 708–15
St. Gregory II, 715–31
St. Gregory III, 731–41
St. Zacharius, 741–52
Stephen II, 752
Stephen III (II), 752–57
St. Paul I, 757–67
Stephen IV (III), 768–72
Adrian I, 772–95
St. Leo III, 795–816
Stephen V (IV), 816–17
St. Paschal I, 817–24
Eugene II, 824–27
Valentine, 827
Gregory IV, 827–44
Sergius II, 844–47
St. Leo IV, 847–55
Benedict III, 855–58
St. Nicholas I, 858–67
Adrian II, 867–72
John VIII, 872–82
Marinus I, 882–84
St. Adrian III, 884–85
Stephen VI (V), 885–91
Formosus, 891–96
Boniface VI, 896
Stephen VII (VI), 896–97
Romanus, 897
Theodore II, 897
John IX, 898–900
Benedict IV, 900–3
Leo V, 903
Sergius III, 904–11
Anastasius III, 911–13
Lando, 913–14
John X, 914–28
Leo VI, 928
Stephen VII (VI), 928–31
John XI, 931–35
Leo VII, 936–39
Stephen IX (VIII), 939–42
Marinus II, 942–46

LIST OF POPES

Agapetus II, 946–55
John XII, 955–64
Leo VIII, 963–65
John XIII, 965–72
Benedict VI, 973–74
Benedict VII, 974–83
John XIV, 983–84
John XV, 985–96
Gregory V, 996–99
Sylvester II, 999–1003
John XVII, 1003
John XVIII, 1004–9
Sergius IV, 1009–12
Benedict VIII, 1012–24
John XIX, 1024–32
Benedict IX, 1032–44, 1045, 1047–48
Damasus II, 1048
St. Leo IX, 1049–54
Victor II, 1055–57
Stephen X (IX), 1057–58
Nicholas II, 1059–61
Alexander II, 1061–73
St. Gregory VII, 1073–85
Victor III, 1086–87
Urban II, 1088–89
Paschal II, 1099–1118
Gelasius II, 1118–19
Calixtus II, 1119–24
Honorius II, 1124–30
Innocent II, 1130–43
Celestine II, 1143–44
Lucius II, 1144–45
Eugene III, 1145–53
Anastasius IV, 1153–54
Adrian IV, 1154–59
Alexander III, 1159–81
Lucius III, 1181–85
Urban III, 1185–87
Gregory VIII, 1187
Clement III, 1187–91
Celestine III, 1191–98
Innocent III, 1198–1216

Honorius III, 1216–27
Gregory IX, 1227–41
Celestine IV, 1241
Innocent IV, 1243–54
Alexander IV, 1254–61
Urban IV, 1261–64
Clement IV, 1265–68
Gregory X, 1271–76
Innocent V, 1276
Adrian V, 1276
John XXI, 1276–77
Nicholas III, 1277–80
Martin IV, 1281–85
Honorius IV, 1285–87
Nicholas IV, 1288–92
St. Celestine V, 1294
Boniface VIII, 1294–1303
Benedict XI, 1303–4
Clement V, 1305–14
John XXII, 1316–34
Benedict XII, 1334–42
Clement VI, 1342–52
Innocent VI, 1352–62
Urban V, 1362–70
Gregory XI, 1370–78
Urban VI, 1378–89
Boniface IX, 1389–1404
Innocent VII, 1404–6
Gregory XII, 1406–15
Martin V, 1417–31
Eugene IV, 1431–47
Nicholas V, 1447–55
Calixtus III, 1455–58
Pius II, 1458–64
Paul II, 1464–71
Sixtus IV, 1471–84
Innocent VIII, 1484–92
Alexander VI, 1492–1503
Pius III, 1503
Julius II, 1503–13
Leo X, 1513–21
Adrian VI, 1522–23
Clement VII, 1523–34

Paul III, 1534–49
Julius III, 1550–55
Marcellus II, 1555
Paul IV, 1555–59
Pius IV, 1559–65
St. Pius V, 1566–72
Gregory XIII, 1572–85
Sixtus V, 1585–90
Urban VII, 1590
Gregory XIV, 1590–91
Innocent IX, 1591
Clement VIII, 1592–1605
Leo XI, 1605
Paul V, 1605–21
Gregory XV, 1621–23
Urban VIII, 1623–44
Innocent X, 1644–55
Alexander VII, 1655–67
Clement IX, 1667–69
Clement X, 1670–76
Innocent XI, 1676–89
Alexander VIII, 1689–91
Innocent XII, 1691–1700
Clement XI, 1700–1721
Innocent XIII, 1721–24
Benedict XIII, 1724–30
Clement XII, 1730–40
Benedict XIV, 1740–58
Clement XIII, 1758–69
Clement XIV, 1769–74
Pius VI, 1775–99
Pius VII, 1800–23
Leo XII, 1823–29
Pius VIII, 1829–30
Gregory XVI, 1831–46
Pius IX, 1846–78
Leo XIII, 1878–1903
Pius X, 1903–14
Benedict XV, 1914–22
Pius XI, 1922–39
Pius XII, 1939–58
John XXIII, 1958–

Bibliography

Abbo, John A., and Hannan, Jerome D. *The Sacred Canons, A Concise Presentation of the Current Disciplinary Norms of the Church.* B. Herder Book Co., St. Louis, Missouri, 1960, revised edition.

Acta Apostolicae Sedis, Annus XXXVIII, Series II, Volume XIII. Typis Polyglottis Vaticanis, 1946.

Aradi, Zsolt. *The Popes, The History of How They Are Chosen, Elected and Crowned.* Farrar, Straus and Cudahy, New York, 1955.

Brusher, Joseph S., S.J. *Popes Through the Ages.* D. Van Nostrand Company, Inc., New York, 1959.

D'Ormesson, Wladimir *The Papacy.* Hawthorn Books, New York, 1959.

Ecclesiastical Review, Volume 115, July-December 1946. "Analecta" article Pages 308-311. Jerome D. Hannan regarding the differences between the Constitution of Pius X, *Vacante Sede Apostolica* of December 25, 1904 and *Vacantis Apostolicae Sedis* of Pius XII of December 8, 1945.

Garrett, Randall. *Pope John XXIII, Pastoral Prince.* Monarch Books, Inc., Derby, Connecticut, 1962.

Gasparri, Cardinal Pietro. *Codex Juris Canonici, Pii X Pontificis Maximi,* iussu digestus Benedicti Papae XV. P. J. Kenedy, New York, 1918.

Giovanetti, Monsignor Alberto. *We Have a Pope.* The Newman Press, Westminster, Maryland, 1959.

Groppi and Lombardi. *Above All a Shepherd, Pope John XXIII.* P. J. Kenedy and Sons, New York, 1959.

Jaeger, Lorenz. *The Ecumenical Council, The Church and Christendom.* P. J. Kenedy and Sons, New York, 1961.

Kittler, Glenn D. *The Papal Princes, A History of the Sacred College of Cardinals.* Funk and Wagnalls, New York, 1960.

Koenig, Reverend Harry C., S. T. D. *Principles for Peace.* National Catholic Welfare Conference, Washington, 1943.

Mater et Magistra, Encyclical Letter of His Holiness Pope John XXIII on Christianity and Social Progress, May 15, 1961. National Catholic Welfare Conference, Washington, 1961.

Nainfa. *Costume of the Prelates of the Catholic Church.* John Murphy Co., Baltimore, 1926.

Pallenberg, Corrado. *Inside the Vatican.* Hawthorn Books, New York, 1960.

Pecher, Eric. *Pope John XXIII*. McGraw-Hill Book Company, New York, 1959.

Perrotta, Paul Christopher, O. P. *Pope John XXIII, His Life and Character*. Thomas Nelson and Sons, New York, 1959.

Pichon, Charles. *The Vatican and Its Role in World Affairs*. E. P. Dutton and Company, New York, 1950.

Reynolds, Robert L. *The Story of the Pope*. Dell Publishing Co., New York, 1957.

Scharp, Heinrich. *How the Catholic Church Is Governed*. Herder and Herder, New York, 1960.

Sugrue, Francis. *Popes in the Modern World*. Thomas Y. Crowell Company, New York, 1961.

INDEX

America, 76, 131
Anacletus, 61
Argentina, 76
Arius of Alexandria, 44
Auriol, President Vincent, 36, 127
Australia, 79
Averulino, Antonio, 61
Avignon, 46

Bacci, Monsignor, 76, 81
Becket, Thomas à, 46
Belgium, 79
Benedict XV, 126
Bergamo, 121, 123, 124, 126
Bernini, Giovanni, 54, 65
Boromeo, St. Charles, 123, 126
Bossuet, Jacques Bénigne, 91
Bramante, 61
Brazil, 76
Brusico, 123
Brussels, 126
Budapest, 28
Bulgaria, 126, 127

Caligula, Emperor, 59
Calvin, John, 46
Canada, 76
Canali, Cardinal, 27
Canterbury Cathedral, 46
Capovilla, Monsignor Loris, 17
Cardinale, Monsignor Ignio, 17, 19, 21, 23
Castel Gandolfo, 27, 51, 75
Ceppetelli, Bishop, 124
Charles VIII, King, 67
Chile, 79
China, 79
Clement IV, 76
Clement VII, 53
Cluny, 45
Colombia, 79
Columbus, Christopher, 17
Constantine, Emperor, 44, 61
Constantinople, 127
Cuba, 79

Dearden, Archbishop John F., 15
Decius, Emperor, 43
Deskur, Monsignor Andrew M., 15, 16, 17
Detroit, 19
Detroit, University of, 16
Diocletian, 43

Ecuador, 79
Egypt, 59
England, 46, 131
Esztergom, 28
Eugenius IV, 61, 63

Fabian, 43
Felici, 15, 21
Fisher, Geoffrey, 131
France, 36, 45, 46, 76, 126, 127

Galerian, Emperor, 44
Garibaldi, Giuseppe, 49
Germany, 46, 76, 131
Greece, 127, 131
Gregory VII, 45, 46
Gregory X, 76

Hadrian IV, 93
Henry II, King, 46
Henry VIII, King, 46
Hildebrand, 45
Hungary, 76

Iakovos, Archbishop, 131
India, 79
Ireland, 79
Italy, 42, 49, 61, 76, 123, 126, 128

Jacob, 39
Jeremiah, 86
Jesus Christ, 39, 42, 44, 54, 61, 71, 81, 85, 87, 91, 95, 121
John XXIII, 15, 17, 19, 21, 22, 23, 24, 25, 27, 36, 37, 44, 95, 115, 117, 123, 124, 128, 130, 131, 133, 134
Joseph, 39

Julius II, 53, 61

Leo XIII, 21
Luther, Martin, 46

Maderna, Carlo, 61
Manzu, Giacomo, 19, 21
Marcellinus, 44
Marelli, Bishop, 126
Michelangelo, 53, 61, 67
Milan, 36, 123, 124
Mindzenty, Cardinal, 28, 76
Montini, Cardinal, 36
Mooney, Archbishop, 28, 76, 81
Munich, 126

New York City, 71
Nicaea, Council of, 44
Noble Guard, 53, 75, 81, 91

O'Connor, Archbishop Martin J., 15
Oriental Rite, 76, 128, 130
Osservatore Romano, 51, 126

Pacelli, Eugenio, 27, 75, 110, 124, 127
Palatine Guard, 53
Palestine, 126
Papal Gendarmes, 53
Papal States, 49
Paris, 126, 127
Paul III, 46
Paul V, 61
Pauline Chapel, 91, 93
Pepin, King, 49
Petain, Marshal, 127
Philip IV, King, 46
Piacenza, 124
"Pietà," 67
Pitocchi, Father Francesco, 124
Pius IX, 44
Pius X, 124, 128
Pius XI, 49, 76, 110
Pius XII, 15, 27, 28, 36, 39, 42, 75, 76, 79, 84, 124, 127
Plautus, 84
Poland, 46, 79
Portugal, 76

Radini-Tedeschi, Bishop, 124, 126

Raphael, 61
Rome, 15, 28, 42, 46, 50, 51, 75, 76, 124, 127, 128
Roncalli, Angelo Giuseppe, 15, 27, 33, 115, 117, 124, 126, 127, 128
Roncalli, Giovanni Battista, 124
Roncalli, Marianna, 124

St. Paul, 63, 67
St. Peter, 27, 49, 54, 61, 63, 65, 67, 72, 75, 76, 81, 87, 117, 126
St. Peter's Basilica, 16, 21, 27, 36, 49, 53, 59, 61, 63, 65, 67, 75, 76, 81
St. Peter's Square, 15, 27, 28, 49, 54, 95
Scotland, 46
Sistine Chapel, 28, 36, 53, 76, 79, 92, 95
Sixtus V, 59
Spain, 76, 126
Spina, Tony, 19, 25
Steiner, Very Reverend Father Celestin J., 16
Stepinac, Cardinal, 28, 76
Swiss Guard, 53, 75, 81, 91
Switzerland, 46

Tien-Ken-Sin, Cardinal, 91
Tisserant, Cardinal Dean Eugene, 81, 92, 117
Trent, 46, 123
Turkey, 127

United Nations, 133
United States, 128
Urban VIII, 61, 65
Urbani, Archbishop, 37

Valeri, Archbishop Valerio, 127
Vatican State, 17, 42, 43, 49, 50, 51, 53, 79, 130, 131
Venice, 33, 36, 37, 117, 121, 128
Verona, 37
Vianney, St. John, 133
Vichy, 127
Villiers, de, Cardinal Jean, 67
Visconti, Theobald, 76
Viterbo, 76

Yugoslavia, 76

Zagreb, 28